FACT AND EXISTENCE

FACT AND EXISTENCE

Proceedings of the
University of Western Ontario
Philosophy Colloquium
1966

Edited by
JOSEPH MARGOLIS

UNIVERSITY OF TORONTO PRESS

© *in this collection Basil Blackwell 1969*
Reprinted in 2018
First published in Canada
and the United States by
University of Toronto Press
1969

ISBN 978-1-4875-8149-7 (paper)
8020 1606 5

PRINTED IN GREAT BRITAIN

FOREWORD

The University of Western Ontario Philosophy Colloquium was inaugurated November, 1966, with the support of The Canada Council and University College, UWO, as the first regular meeting of professional philosophers convened on Canadian soil, drawn from the entire English-speaking world. We had hoped to provide (and believe we succeeded in providing) a Canadian setting for exchanges among specialists, that would serve at once as a high international forum at home and as an introduction abroad of the work of Canadian professionals.

The formal papers included in this our first series, under the heading 'Fact and Existence', have been duly revised since their presentation at the Colloquium. Also, in a number of instances, it has proved useful to include some comments from the floor on particular issues, to which the initial symposium speakers have expressed a wish to respond; their Replies have been addressed as well to their commentators, in the interest of rounding out the exchange.

Thanks are due particularly to the Director of The Canada Council, M. J. Boucher and to Dean A. W. Trueman, University College, for affording us the opportunity to launch a promising new venture.

J.M.

London, Ontario
February 1, 1968

CONTENTS

	page
Foreword	v

Address: Existence and Quantification
   W. V. Quine, *Harvard University*   1

Symposium: Descartes' Ontological Argument
   Anthony Kenny, *Balliol College, Oxford*   18
   Norman Malcolm, *Cornell University*   36
   Terence Penelhum, *University of Calgary*   43
   Comments:
      Bernard Williams, *King's College, Cambridge*   55
      E. Sosa, *Brown University*   56
   Reply, by Anthony Kenny   58

Symposium: On Events and Event-Descriptions
   R. M. Martin, *New York University*   63
   Donald Davidson, *Princeton University*   74
   R. J. Butler, *University of Waterloo*   84
   Comment:
      Wesley C. Salmon, *Indiana University*   95
   Reply, by R. M. Martin   97

Symposium: Existence-Assumptions in Practical Thinking
   S. Körner, *University of Bristol*   110
   J. J. Thomson, *Massachusetts Institute of Technology*   123
   Bernard Williams, *King's College, Cambridge*   132
   Reply, by S. Körner   142

ADDRESS

EXISTENCE AND QUANTIFICATION

W. V. QUINE

The question whether there are numbers, or qualities, or classes, is a metaphysical question, such as the logical positivists have regarded as meaningless. On the other hand the question whether there are rabbits, or unicorns, is as meaningful as can be. A conspicuous difference is that bodies can be perceived. Still, this is not all that matters; for we can evidently say also, meaningfully and without metaphysics, that there are prime numbers between 10 and 20.

What typifies the metaphysical cases is rather, according to an early doctrine of Carnap's,[1] the use of category words, or *Allwörter*. It is meaningful to ask whether there are prime numbers between 10 and 20, but meaningless to ask in general whether there are numbers; and likewise it is meaningful to ask whether there are rabbits, or unicorns, but meaningless to ask in general whether there are bodies.

But this ruling is unsatisfactory in two ways. The first difficulty is that there is no evident standard of what to count as a category, or category word. Typically, in terms of formalized quantification theory, each category comprises the range of some distinctive style of variables. But the style of variable is an arbitrary matter, and surely of no help in distinguishing between meaningful questions of existence and metaphysical questions of existence. For there are no external constraints on styles of variables; we can use distinctive styles for different sorts of number, or a single style for all sorts of numbers and everything else as well. Notations with one style of variables and notations with many are intertranslatable.

There is another idea of category that may superficially seem more profound. It is the idea of semantic category, as Leśniewski called it,[2] or what linguists call a substitution class. Expressions

[1] Rudolf Carnap, *Logical Syntax of Language*, p. 292.
[2] Stanisław Leśniewski, 'Grundzüge eines neuen Systems der Grundlagen der Mathematik', §§ 1–11, *Fundamenta Mathematicae* 14 (1929), pp. 1–81.

belong to the same substitution class if, whenever you put one for the other in a meaningful sentence, you get a meaningful sentence. The question whether numbers constitute a category gives way, in these terms, to a question of the meaningfulness of the sentences that we obtain by supplanting number words by other words. However, what to count as meaningful is not at all clear. The empirical linguist manages the point after a fashion by considering what sentences could be elicited by reasonable means from naive native speakers. But such a criterion is of little value to a philosopher with a reform programme. In fact, the question what existence sentences to count as meaningless was where we came in.

Existence questions were ruled meaningless by Carnap when they turned on category words. This was, I said, an unsatisfactory ruling in two respects. We have seen one of the respects: the tenuousness of the idea of category word. Now the other respect is that anyway sense needs to be made of categorial existence questions, however you choose your categories. For it can happen in the austerest circles that some one will try to rework a mathematical system in such a way as to avoid assuming certain sorts of objects. He may try to get by with the assumption of just numbers and not sets of numbers; or he may try to get by with classes to the exclusion of properties; or he may try, like Whitehead, to avoid points and make do with extended regions and sets of regions. Clearly the system-maker in such cases is trying for something, and there is some distinction to be drawn between his getting it and not.

When he want to check on existence, bodies have it over other objects on the score of their perceptibility. But we have moved now to the question of checking not on existence, but on imputations of existence: on what a theory says exists. The question is when to maintain that a theory assumes a given object, or objects of a given sort—numbers, say, or sets of numbers, or properties, or points. To show that a theory assumes a given object, or objects of a given class, we have to show that the theory would be false if that object did not exist, or if that class were empty; hence that the theory requires that object, or members of that class, in order to be true. How are such requirements revealed?

Perhaps we find proper names of the objects. Still, this is no evidence that the objects are required, except as we can show that these proper names of the objects are used in the theory *as* proper names of the objects. The word 'dog' may be used as a proper name of an animal species, but it may also be used merely as a general term true of each of various individuals and naming no one object at all; so the presence of the word is of itself no evidence that species are being assumed as objects. Again even 'Pegasus', which is inflexibly a proper name grammatically speaking, can be used by persons who deny existence of its object. It is even used in denying that existence.

What would count then as evidence that an expression is used in a theory as a name of an object? Let us represent the expression as 'a'. Now if the theory affirms the existentially quantified identity '$(\exists x)(x=a)$', certainly we have our answer: 'a' is being used to name an object. In general we may say that an expression is used in a theory as naming if and only if the existentially quantified identity built on that expression is true according to the theory.

Of course we could also say, more simply, that 'a' is used to name an object if and only if the statement 'a exists' is true for the theory. This is less satisfactory only insofar as the meaning of 'exists' may have seemed less settled than quantifiers and identity. We may indeed take '$(\exists x)(x=a)$' as explicating 'a exists'. John Bacon has noted a nice parallel here:[3] just as 'a eats' is short for 'a eats something', so 'a is' is short for 'a is something'.

An expression 'a' may occur in a theory, we saw, with or without purporting to name an object. What clinches matters is rather the quantification '$(\exists x)(x=a)$'. It is the existential quantifier, not the 'a' itself, that carries existential import. This is just what existential quantification is for, of course. It is a logically regimented rendering of the 'there is' idiom. The bound variable 'x' ranges over the universe, and the existential quantification says that at least one of the objects in the universe satisfies the appended condition—in this case the condition of being the object a. To show that some given object is required in a theory, what we have to show is no more nor less than that that object is required, for the truth of the theory, to be among the values over which the bound variables range.

Appreciation of this point affords us more than an explication of 'a exists', since the existentially quantified identity '$(\exists x)(x=a)$'

[3] John Bennett Bacon, *Being and Existence*, dissertation, Yale, 1966.

is one case of existential quantification among many. It is a case where the value of the variable that is said to exist is an object with a name; the name is 'a'. This is the way with singular existence sentences generally, sentences of the form 'a exists' or 'There is such a thing as a', but it is not the way with existence sentences generally. For instance, under classical set theory there are, given any interpreted notation, some real numbers that are not separately specifiable in that notation. The existence sentence 'There are unspecifiable real numbers' is true, and expressible as an existential quantification; but the values of the variable that account for the truth of this quantification are emphatically not objects with names. Here then is another reason why quantified variables, not names, are what to look to for the existential force of a theory.

Another way of saying what objects a theory requires is to say that they are the objects that some of the predicates of the theory have to be true of, in order for the theory to be true. But this is the same as saying that they are the objects that have to be values of the variables in order for the theory to be true. It is the same, anyway, if the notation of the theory includes for each predicate a complementary predicate, its negation. For then, given any value of a variable, some predicate is true of it; viz., any predicate or its complement. And conversely, of course, whatever a predicate is true of is a value of variables. Predication and quantification, indeed, are intimately linked; for a predicate is simply any expression that yields a sentence, an open sentence, when adjoined to one or more quantifiable variables. When we schematize a sentence in the predicative way 'Fa', or 'a is an F', our recognition of an 'a' part and an 'F' part turns strictly on our use of variables of quantification; the 'a' represents a part of the sentence that stands where a quantifiable variable could stand, and the 'F' represents the rest.

Our question was: what objects does a theory require? Our answer is: those objects that have to be values of variables for the theory to be true. Of course a theory may, in this sense, require no objects in particular, and still not tolerate an empty universe of discourse either, for the theory might be fulfilled equally by either of two mutually exclusive universes. If for example the theory implies '$(\exists x)$ (x is a dog)', it will not tolerate an empty universe; still the theory might be fulfilled by a universe that contained collies to the exclusion of spaniels, and also vice versa. So there is more to be said of a theory, ontologically, than just saying what objects, if any, the theory requires; we can also ask what various universes would be severally sufficient. The specific objects required, if any, are the objects common to all those universes.

I think mainly of single-sorted quantification; i.e., a single style of variables. As remarked, the many-sorted is translatable into one-sorted. Generally such translation has the side effect of admitting as meaningful some erstwhile meaningless predications. E.g., if the predicate 'divisible by 3' is henceforth to be trained on general variables instead of number variables, we must make sense of calling things other than numbers divisible by 3. But this is easy; we may count such attributions false instead of meaningless. In general, thus, the reduction of many-sorted quantification to one-sorted has the effect of merging some substitution classes; more words become meaningfully interchangeable.

Carnap's reservations over *Allwörter* now cease to apply, and so his special strictures against philosophical questions of existence lapse as well. To what extent have we meanwhile become clearer on such questions of existence? On the higher-order question, what things a theory assumes there to be, we have gained a pointer: look to the behavior of quantified variables and don't cavil about names. Regarding the meaning of existence itself our progress is less clear.

Existence is what existential quantification expresses. There are things of kind F if and only if $(\exists x) Fx$. This is as unhelpful as it is undebatable, since it is how one explains the symbolic notation of quantification to begin with. The fact is that it is unreasonable to ask for an explication of existence in simpler terms. We found an explication of singular existence, 'a exists', as '$(\exists x)(x=a)$'; but explication in turn of the existential quantifier itself, 'there is', 'there are', explication of general existence, is a forlorn cause. Further understanding we may still seek even here, but not in the form of explication. We may still ask what counts as evidence for existential quantifications.

To this question there is no simple, general answer. If the open sentence under the quantifier is something like 'x is a rabbit' or 'x is a unicorn', then the evidence, if any, is largely the testimony of the senses. If the open sentence is 'x is a prime number between

10 and 20', the evidence lies in computation. If the open sentence is merely '*x* is a number', or '*x* is a class', or the like, the evidence is much harder to pinpoint. But I think the positivists were mistaken when they despaired of evidence in such cases and accordingly tried to draw up boundaries that would exclude such sentences as meaningless. Existence statements in this philosophical vein do admit of evidence, in the sense that we can have reasons, and essentially scientific reasons, for including numbers or classes or the like in the range of values of our variables. And other existence statements in this metaphysical vein can be subject to counter-evidence; we can have essentially scientific reasons for excluding propositions, perhaps, or attributes, or unactualized bodies, from the range of our variables. Numbers and classes are favoured by the power and facility which they contribute to theoretical physics and other systematic discourse about nature. Propositions and attributes are disfavoured by some irregular behaviour in connection with identity and substitution. Considerations for and against existence are more broadly systematic, in these philosophical examples, than in the case of rabbits or unicorns or prime numbers between 10 and 20; but I am persuaded that the difference is a matter of degree. Our theory of nature grades off from the most concrete fact to speculations about the curvature of space-time, or the continuous creation of hydrogen atoms in an expanding universe; and our evidence grades off correspondingly, from specific observation to broadly systematic considerations. Existential quantifications of the philosophical sort belong to the same inclusive theory and are situated way out at the end, farthest from observable fact.

Thus far I have been playing down the difference between commonsense existence statements, as of rabbits and unicorns, and philosophical existence statements, as of numbers and attributes. But there is also a curious difference between commonsense existence statements and philosophical ones that needs to be played up, and it is one that can be appreciated already right in among the rabbits. For let us reflect that a theory might accommodate all rabbit data and yet admit as values of its variables no rabbits or other bodies but only qualities, times, and places. The adherents of that theory, or *immaterialists*, would have a sentence which, as a whole, had the same stimulus meaning as our sentence 'There is a rabbit in the yard'; yet in the quantificational sense of the words they would have to deny that there is a rabbit in the yard or anywhere else. Here, then, prima facie, are two senses of existence of rabbits, a common sense and a philosophical sense.

A similar distinction can be drawn in the case of the prime numbers between 10 and 20. Suppose someone has for reasons of nominalism renounced most of mathematics and settled for bodies as sole values of his variables. He can still do such part of arithmetic as requires no variables. In particular he can still subscribe to the nine-clause alternation '11 is prime or 12 is prime or 13 is prime or . . . or 19 is prime'. In this sense he agrees with us that there are primes between 10 and 20, but in the quantificational sense he denies that there are primes or numbers at all.

Shall we say: so much the worse for a quantificational version of existence? Hardly; we already found this version trivial but undebatable. Are there then two senses of existence? Only in a derivative way. For us common men who believe in bodies and prime numbers, the statements 'There is a rabbit in the yard' and 'There are prime numbers between 10 and 20' are free from double talk. Quantification does them justice. When we come to the immaterialist, and we tell him there is a rabbit in the yard, he will know better than to demur on account of his theory; he will acquiesce on account of a known holophrastic relation of stimulus synonymy between our sentence and some sentence geared to his different universe. In practice he will even stoop to our idiom himself, both to facilitate communication and because of speech habits lingering from his own benighted youth. This he will do when the theoretical question is not at issue, just as we speak of the sun as rising. Insofar we may say, I grant, that there are for him two senses of existence; but there is no confusion, and the theoretical use is rather to be respected as literal and basic than deplored as a philosophical disorder.

Similar remarks apply to our nominalist. He will agree that there are primes between 10 and 20, when we are talking arithmetic and not philosophy. When we turn to philosophy he will condone that usage as a mere manner of speaking, and offer the paraphrase. Similar remarks apply to us; many of our casual remarks in the 'there are' form would want dusting up when our thoughts turn seriously ontological. Each time, if a point is made of it, the burden is of course on us to paraphrase or retract.

It has been fairly common in philosophy early and late to distinguish between being, as the broadest concept, and existence, as narrower. This is no distinction of mine; I mean 'exists' to cover all there is, and such of course is the force of the quantifier. For those who do make the distinction, the existent tends to be on the concrete or temporal side. Now there was perhaps a reminder of the distinction in the case of the rabbit and the immaterialist. At that point two senses of 'there is', a common and a philosophical, threatened to diverge. Perhaps the divergence which that sort of case suggests has been one factor in making philosophers receptive to a distinction between existence and being. Anyway, it ought not to. For the point there was that the rabbit was not a value of the immaterialist's variables; thus existence, if this were the analogy, would not be a species of being. Moreover, we saw that the sensible materiality of the rabbit was inessential to the example, since the prime numbers between 10 and 20 sustained much the same point.

Along with the annoying practice of restricting the term 'existence' to a mere species of what there is, there is Meinong's bizarre deviation of an opposite kind. *Gegenstände* or objects, for him, comprised more even than what there was; an object might or might not be. His notion of object was, as Chisholm puts it, *jenseits von Sein und Nichtsein*.[4] Oddly enough, I find this idea a good one, provided that we bolster it with Bentham's theory of fictions. Contextual definition, or what Bentham called paraphrasis, can enable us to talk very considerably and conveniently about putative objects without footing an ontological bill. It is a strictly legitimate way of making theories in which there is less than meets the eye.

Bentham's idea of paraphrasis flowered late, in Russell's theory of descriptions. Russell's theory affords a rigorous and important example of how expressions can be made to parade as names and then be explained away as a mere manner of speaking, by explicit paraphrase of the context into an innocent notation. However, Russell's theory of descriptions was less a way of simulating objects than of contextually defining terms to designate real objects. When the description fails to specify anything, Russell accommodates it grudgingly: he makes its immediate sentential contexts uniformly false.

[4] Roderick M. Chisholm, 'Jenseits von Sein und Nichtsein', K. S. Guthke ed., *Dichtung und Deutung*, Bern and Munich: Francke, 1961.

Where we find Russell exploiting paraphrasis for simulation of objects is not in his theory of descriptions but rather in his contextual theory of classes. There are really no such things as classes, according to him, but he simulates discourse about classes by contextual definition, and not grudgingly; not just by making all immediate contexts false.

There is a well-known catch to Russell's theory of classes. The theory depends on an unheralded but irreducible assumption of attributes as values of bound variables. Russell only reduces classes to attributes, and this can scarcely be viewed as a reduction in the right direction unless for wrong reasons.

But it is possible by paraphrasis to introduce a certain amount of class talk, less than Russell's, without really assuming attributes or any other objects beyond the ones wanted as members of the simulated classes. I developed this line somewhat under the head of virtual classes, long ago, and Richard Martin was at it independently at that time.[5] Lately I made much use of it in *Set Theory and Its Logic*. What it yields is substantial enough to implant new hopes, in many breasts, of making do with a nominalist ontology. Unfortunately these would have to be breasts unmindful of the needs of mathematics. For of itself the virtual theory of classes affords no adequate foundation for the classical mathematics even of the positive integers. However, it is handy still as a supplementary technique after we have bowed to the need of assuming real classes too; for it enables us to simulate further classes beyond those assumed. For that reason, and also because I think it good strategy in all subjects to postpone assumptions until needed, I am in favour of exploiting the virtual theory for all it is worth.

Virtual classes do not figure as values of bound variables. They owe their utility partly to a conventional use of schematic letters, which, though not quantifiable, behave like free variables. The simulated names of the virtual classes are substitutable for such letters. We could even call these letters free variables, if we resist the temptation to bind them. Virtual classes can then be seen as simulated values of these simulated variables. Hintikka has presented a logic, not specifically of classes but of entities and non-entities generally, in which the non-entities figure thus as

---

[5] R. M. Martin, 'A homogeneous system of formal logic', *Journal of Symbolic Logic* 8 (1943), pp. 1–23.

values only of free variables.⁶ Or, to speak less figuratively, the singular terms which fail to designate can be substituted only for free variables, whereas singular terms which do designate can be used also in instantiating quantification.

So much for simulated objects. I want now to go back and pick up a loose end where we were considering the immaterialist. I said he would fall in with our statement 'There is a rabbit in the yard' just to convey agreement on the stimulus content, or even out of habit carried over from youth. But what about the alternative situation where the immaterialist is not a deviant Western intellectual, but a speaker of an unknown language which we are bent on construing? Suddenly the conditions themselves become problematical. In principle there is no difficulty in equating a sentence of his holophrastically, by stimulus meaning, with our sentence 'There is a rabbit in the yard'. But how could it ever be determined, even in probabilistic terms, that his ontology includes qualities, times, and places and excludes bodies? I argued in *Word and Object* that such ontological questions regarding a radically alien language make no objective sense. In principle we could devise any of various sets of analytical hypotheses for translating the language into ours; many such sets can conform fully to all evidence and even be behaviourally equivalent to one another, and yet disagree with one another as to the native's equivalents of our predicates and quantifiers. For practical translation we fix on one of the adequate sets of analytical hypotheses, and in the light of it we report even on the native's ontology; but what to report is uniquely determined neither by evidence nor by fact. There is no fact of the matter.

Consider, in contrast, the truth functions. We can state substantial behavioural conditions for interpreting a native sentence connective as, say, alternation. The requirement is that the natives be disposed to dissent from any compound statement, formed by the connective in question, when and only when disposed to dissent from each of the component statements, and that they be disposed to assent to the compound whenever disposed to assent to a component. These conditions remain indeed less

⁶ Jaakko Hintikka, 'Existential presuppositions and existential commitments', *Journal of Philosophy* 56 (1959), pp. 125–137. For a bigger venture in this direction see Henry S. Leonard, 'Essences, attributes, and predicates', *Proceedings and Addresses of the American Philosophical Association* 37 (1964), pp. 25–51.

than definitive on one point: on the question of a native's assenting to the compound but to neither component. For instance we may affirm of two horses that one or the other will win, and still not be prepared to affirm of either one that he will win.[7] Still, the two conditions do much toward identifying alternation; more than any behavioural conditions can do for quantification. And it is easy to do as well for the other truth functions as for alternation.

There is indeed a variant of quantification, favoured by Leśniewski[2] and by Ruth Marcus,[8] which does admit behavioural criteria of translation as substantial as those for the truth functions. I shall call it *substitutional* quantification. An existential substitutional quantification is counted as true if and only if there is an expression which, when substituted for the variable, makes the open sentence after the quantifier come out true. A universal quantification is counted as true if no substitution makes the open sentence come out false. Behavioural conditions for interpreting a native construction as existential substitutional quantification, then, are readily formulated. We fix on parts of the construction as candidates for the roles of quantifier and variable; then a condition of their fitness is that the natives be disposed to dissent from a whole quantified sentence when and only when disposed to dissent from each of the sentences obtainable by dropping the quantifier and substituting for the variable. A second condition is that the natives be disposed to assent to the whole whenever disposed to assent to one of the sentences obtainable by dropping the quantifier and substituting for the variable. As in the case of alternation, the behavioural conditions do not wholly settle assent; but they go far. Analogous criteria for universal substitutional quantification are equally evident.

Naturally we never expect mathematical certainty as to whether such a behavioural criterion is fulfilled by a given construction in the native language. For any one choice of native locutions as candidates for the role of quantifier and variable, an infinite lot of quantified sentences and substitution instances would have to be tested. The behavioural criteria for the truth functions are similar in this respect. Empirical induction is all we have to go on, and all we would ask.

---

[7] In *Word and Object*, Cambridge: M.I.T. Press, 1960, p. 58, I gave only the condition on dissent and so overlooked this limitation on the assent side. Conjunction suffered in equal and opposite fashion.

[8] Ruth B. Marcus, 'Modalities and intensional languages', *Synthèse* 13 (1961), pp. 303–322.

Substitutional quantification and the truth functions are, in brief, far and away more recognizable behaviourally than classical quantification, or what we may call *objectual* quantification. We can locate objectual quantification in our own language because we grow up using those very words: if not the actual quantifiers, then words like 'exists' and 'there is' by which they come to be explained to us. We can locate it in other languages only relative to chosen or inherited codes of translation which are in a sense arbitrary. They are arbitrary in the sense that they could be materially different and still conform to all the same behaviour apart from the behaviour of translation itself. Objectual quantification is in this sense more parochial than substitutional quantification and the truth functions.

In his substitutional quantification Leśniewski used different styles of variables for different substitution classes. Substitutional quantification in the substitution class of singular terms, or names, is the sort that comes closest to objectual quantification. But it is clearly not equivalent to it—not unless each of our objects is specifiable by some singular term or other in our language, and no term of that substitution class fails to specify an object. For this reason substitutional quantification gives no acceptable version of existence properly so-called, not if objectual quantification does. Moreover, substitutional quantification makes good sense, explicable in terms of truth and substitution, no matter what substitution class we take—even that whose sole member is the left-hand parenthesis.[9] To conclude that entities are being assumed that trivially, and that far out, is simply to drop ontological questions. Nor can we introduce any control by saying that only substitutional quantification in the substitution class of singular terms is to count as a version of existence. We just now saw one reason for this, and there is another: the very notion of singular term appeals implicitly to classical or objectual quantification. This is the point that I made earlier about analyzing sentences according to the scheme '*Fa*'. Leśniewski did not himself relate his kind of quantification to ontological commitments.

This does not mean that theories using substitutional quantification and no objectual quantification can get on *without* objects. I hold rather that the question of the ontological commitment of a theory does not properly arise except as that theory is expressed

[9] Leśniewski's example, from a conversation of 1933 in Warsaw.

in classical quantificational form, or insofar as one has in mind how to translate it into that form. I hold this for the simple reason that the existential quantifier, in the objectual sense, is given precisely the existential interpretation and no other: there are things which are thus and so.

It is easy to see how substitutional quantification might be translated into a theory of standard form. Consider a substitutional quantification whose quantifier is existential and contains the variable v and governs the open sentence S. We can paraphrase it in syntactical and semantical terms, with objectual quantification, thus: there is an expression which, put for v in S, yields a truth. Universal quantification can be handled similarly. For this method the theory into which we translate is one that talks about expressions of the original theory, and assumes them among its objects—as values of its variables of objectual quantification. By arithmetized syntax, natural numbers would do as well. Thus we may look upon substitutional quantification not as avoiding all ontological commitment, but as getting by with, in effect, a universe of natural numbers.

Substitutional quantification has its points. If I could see my way to getting by with an all-purpose universe whose objects were denumerable and indeed enumerated, I would name each object numerically and settle for substitutional quantification. I would consider this an advance epistemologically, since substitutional quantification is behaviourally better determined than objectual quantification. Here then is a new reason, if one were needed, for aspiring to a denumerable universe.

In switching at that point to substitutional quantification we would not, as already stressed, reduce our denumerable universe to a null universe. We would, however, turn our backs on ontological questions. Where substitutional quantification serves, ontology lacks point. The ontology of such a theory is worth trying to elicit only when we are making translations or other comparisons between that theory and a theory which, because of an indenumerable or indefinite universe, is irreducibly committed to something like objectual quantification. Indenumerable and indefinite universes are what, in the end, give point to objectual quantification and ontology.[10]

[10] The foregoing reflections on substitutional quantification were elicited largely by discussions with Burton Dreben. On the pointlessness of ontology at the denumerable level see also my *The Ways of Paradox*, New York: Random House, 1966, p. 203.

I urged that objectual quantification, more than substitutional quantification, is in a sense parochial. Then so is the idea of being; for objectual existential quantification was devised outright for 'there is'. But still one may ask, and Hao Wang has asked, whether we do not represent being in an unduly parochial way when we equate it strictly with our own particular quantification theory to the exclusion of somewhat deviant quantification theories. Substitutional quantification indeed would not serve as an account of being, for reasons already noted; but what of intuitionistic quantification theory, or other deviations?[11] Now one answer is that it would indeed be a reasonable use of words to say that the intuitionist has a different doctrine of being from mine, as he has a different quantification theory; and that I am simply at odds with the intuitionist on the one as on the other. When I try to determine the universe of someone else's theory, I use 'being' my way. In particular thus I might come out with a different inventory of an intuitionist's universe then the intuitionist, with his deviant sense of being, would come out with. Or I might simply see no satisfactory translation of his notation into mine, and so conclude that the question of his ontology cannot be raised in terms acceptable to me.

But this answer misses an important element in Wang's question. Namely, how much better than arbitrary is our particular quantification theory, seen as one in some possible spectrum of quantification theories? Misgivings in this direction can be fostered by noting the following form of sentence, due essentially to Henkin:[12]

(1) Each thing bears P to something y and each thing bears Q to something w such that Ryw.

The best we can do for this in ordinary quantificational terms is:

(2) $(x)(\exists y)(Pxy . (z)(\exists w)(Qzw . Ryw))$.

or equally:

(3) $(z)(\exists w)(Qzw . (x)(\exists y)(Pxy . Ryw))$.

These are not equivalent. (2) represents the choice of y as independent of z; (3) does not. (3) represents the choice of w as independent of x; (2) does not. Moreover there are inter-

---

[11] One such, propounded by Leonard, p. 39, combines substitutional and objectual quantification.

[12] Leon Henkin, 'Some remarks on infinitely long formulas', *Infinitistic Methods* (proceedings of a Warsaw symposium), New York: Pergamon, 1961, pp. 167–183; specifically, p. 181.

pretations of 'P', 'Q', and 'R' in (1) that make both dependences gratuitous; for instance, interpretation of 'P' as 'is part of', 'Q' as 'contains', and 'R' as 'is bigger than'.

(4) Each thing is part of something y and each thing contains something z such that y is bigger than z.

One may suspect that the notation of quantification is at fault in forcing a choice between (2) and (3) in a case like this.

By admitting functions as values of our bound variables, Henkin observes, we can escape the limitations of (2) and (3) as follows:

(5) $(\exists f)\,(\exists g)\,(x)\,(z)\,(Pxf_x \,.\, Qzg_z \,.\, Rf_x g_z)$.

But this move assumes higher-order objects, which may seem out of keeping with the elementary character of (1). Henkin then points out a liberalization of the classical quantification notation which does the work of (5) without quantifying over functions. Just allow branching quantifiers, thus:

(6) $\begin{matrix}(x)\,(\exists y)\\ (z)\,(\exists w)\end{matrix}$ $(Pxy \,.\, Qzw \,.\, Ryw)$.

One may feel, therefore, that an ontological standard geared to classical quantification theory is over-critical. It would interpret (4) as assuming functions, by interpreting it as (5), whereas the deviant quantification theory with its branching quantifiers would interpret (4) more plausibly as not talking of any functions. And it would do so without slipping into the inappropriate bias of (2), or that of (3).

One is tempted farther by the following considerations. The second-order formula (5) is of a kind that I shall call *functionally existential*, meaning that all its function quantifiers are out in front and existential. Now there is a well-known complete proof procedure of Skolem's for classical quantification theory, which consists in showing a formula inconsistent by taking what I call its functional normal form and deriving a truth-functional contradiction from it.[13] Anyone familiar with the procedure can quickly see that it works not only for all first-order formulas, that is, all formulas in the notation of classical quantification theory, but all these functionally existential formulas as well. Any inconsistent formula not only of classical quantification theory, but of this functionally existential annex, can be shown inconsistent by one

[13] See my *Selected Logic Papers*, New York: Random House, 1966, pp. 196 ff.

and the same method of functional normal forms. This makes the annex seem pretty integral. One is tempted to seek further notational departures, in the first-orderish spirit of the branching quantifiers, which would suffice to accommodate all the functionally existential formulas the way (6) accommodates (5). Henkin has in fact devised a general notation of this kind.

By considerations of duality, moreover, these reflections upon functionally existential formulas can be paralleled with regard to functionally universal formulas—those whose function quantifiers are out in front and universal. Skolem's method of proving inconsistency has as its dual a method of proving validity, and it works not only for all first-order formulas but for all these functionally universal formulas as well. Thus this still further annex would be every bit as integral as the functionally existential one. We seem to see our way, then, to so enlarging classical quantification theory as to gain all the extra power that would have been afforded by assuming functions, so long as the function quantifiers were out in front and all existential or all universal. It would mean a grateful slackening of our ontological accountability.

These reflections encourage the idea that our classical logic of quantification is arbitrarily restrictive. However, I shall now explain what I think to be a still weightier counter-consideration. The classical logic of quantification has a complete proof procedure for validity and a complete proof procedure for inconsistency; indeed each procedure serves both purposes, since a formula is valid if and only if its negation is inconsistent. The most we can say for the functionally existential annex, on the other hand, is that it has a complete proof procedure for inconsistency; and the most we can say for the functionally universal annex is that it has a complete proof procedure for validity. The trick of proving a formula valid by proving its negation inconsistent, or vice versa, is not applicable in the annexes, since in general the negation of a functionally existential formula is not equivalent to a functionally existential formula (but only to a functionally universal one), and conversely. In fact there is a theorem due to Craig[14] which shows that the negation of a functionally existential formula is never equivalent to a functionally existential formula, unless the functions were superfluous and the formula was equivalent to a

---

[14] William Craig, 'Three uses of the Herbrand-Gentzen theorem', *Journal of Symbolic Logic* 22 (1956), pp. 269–285; specifically p. 281.

first-order formula; and correspondingly for functionally universal formulas. Thus classical, unsupplemented quantification theory is on this score maximal: it is as far out as you can go and still have complete coverage of validity and inconsistency by the Skolem proof procedure.

Henkin even shows that the valid formulas which are quantified merely in the fourfold fashion shown in (5), or (6), are already more than can be covered by any proof procedure, at any rate when identity is included.[15]

Here then is a reason to draw boundaries in such a way as to regard (6) as talking covertly of functions after all, and as receiving a just analysis in (5). On this view (1) is not the proper business of pure quantification theory after all, but treats of functions. That is, if the form (1) is not to be read with the bias (2) or the bias (3), it is to be explained as (5).

We may be somewhat reconciled to this conclusion by an observation of Jean van Heijenoort, to the effect that (1) is not after all very ordinary language; its grammar is doubtful. Can the 'such that' reach back across the 'and' to cover the 'y'? If assignment of meaning to extraordinary language is what we are about, we may indeed assign (5) and not wonder at its being irreducibly of second order.

Since introducing (1), I have proved nothing. I have explained two sorts of considerations, one to illustrate how we might be led to see the classical state of quantification theory as arbitrary, and the other to illustrate how it is better than arbitrary. Classical quantification theory enjoys an extraordinary combination of depth and simplicity, beauty and utility. It is bright within and bold in its boundaries. Deviations from it are likely, in contrast, to look rather arbitrary. But insofar as they exist it seems clearest and simplest to say that deviant concepts of existence exist along with them.

[15] P. 182 and footnote. Henkin derives this conclusion from a theorem of Mostowski by an argument which he credits to Ehrenfeucht.
   I am indebted to Peter Geach for first bringing the question of (1) to my attention, in January 1960; and I am indebted to my colleagues Burton Dreben and Saul Kripke and my pupil Christopher Hill for steering me to pertinent papers. Dreben's advice has been helpful also elsewhere.

Symposium I

DESCARTES' ONTOLOGICAL ARGUMENT

ANTHONY KENNY*

I

In the *Discourse of Method*, Descartes says: 'I saw quite well that, assuming a triangle, its three angles must be equal to two right angles; but for all that I saw nothing that assured me that there was any triangle in the real world. On the other hand, going back to an examination of my idea of a perfect Being, I found that this included the existence of such a Being; in the same way as the idea of a triangle includes the equality of its three angles to two right angles, or the idea of a sphere includes the equidistance of all parts (of its surface) from the centre; or indeed, in an even more evident way. Consequently it is at least as certain that God, the perfect Being in question, is or exists, as any proof in geometry can be' (IV).

Let us take the steps of this proof in turn. What is meant by 'assuming a triangle'? (*Supposant une triangle*). Does it mean: assuming some triangle exists? M. Gilson glosses: 'the supposition that a triangle be given, whether it exist really or not' and appeals to the Latin text: *si exempli causa supponamus dari aliquod triangulum*. But so far as this text goes, we seem to have two alternatives: (1) If a triangle exists, it has its three angles equal to two right angles. (2) Any triangle, whether it exists or not, has its three angles equal to two right angles.

We may notice that neither of these formulations can be translated into Frege-Russell notation; and we may notice, too, as Descartes says, that neither contains any assurance 'that there is any triangle in the real world'.

Further light is thrown on Descartes' meaning by a passage in the Fifth Meditation. 'When I imagine a triangle, it may be that no such figure exists anywhere outside my thought, or never has

* The greater part of this paper appeared with some modification as a chapter in *Descartes: A Study of his Philosophy* by Anthony Kenny, © copyright 1968 by Random House, Inc. and is reprinted by permission of the publisher.

existed; but there certainly is its determinate nature, its essence, its form (*est tamen profecto determinata quaedam eius natura, sive essentia, sive forma*), which is unchangeable and eternal. This is no figment of mine, and does not depend on my mind, as is clear from the following: various properties can be proved of this triangle, e.g. that its three angles are together equal to two right angles, that its greatest side subtends its greatest angle, and so on' (AT [Adam et Tannery] VII, 64). He says (a little above) that this is an example of 'things which, even if they perhaps exist nowhere outside me, cannot be said to be nothing'.

This passage, by substituting for the phrase 'to be in the world' of the *Discourse* the phrase 'exist outside my thought', brings in by implicit contrast the notion of 'existence in thought'. Moreover, unlike the *Discourse* passage, it distinguishes between the triangle, on the one hand, and the nature or essence or form of the triangle on the other. Further, it adds a more fortunate example of an eternal and immutable property of a triangle than the one Descartes uses in setting forth the ontological argument. Since the development of non-Euclidean geometries it is no longer true to say that the three angles of a triangle must equal two right angles. Some would say this reveals, at this point, a fundamental misconception of Descartes concerning the nature of geometry; to me it seems to show simply that he chose a poor example of what he had in mind. His second example is better: even of non-Euclidean triangles it is true that the greatest side subtends the greatest angle. It would be possible, I think, to safeguard Descartes from criticism on this point by substituting this example for the other one wherever it occurs in his statement of his proof. But I will not do so, but will proceed as if it were a geometrical truth that the three angles of any triangle equal two right angles.

It is clear, I think, that what Descartes means by a triangle existing in the world, or existing outside thought, is for there to be in the world some body which has a triangular shape. Clearly, someone who is in doubt whether any body exists at all does not know whether, in this sense, any triangle exists in the world. But the supposition that no triangles exist in the world is not merely a part of Descartes' hyperbolical doubt. He believed the supposition to be true of the macroscopic world even after he had provided the solution to his methodic doubts. 'I do not agree that these [geometric figures] have ever fallen under our senses, as everyone normally believes, because though there is no doubt that there could be in the world figures such as the geometers consider, I deny that there are any around us, unless perhaps they be so small that they make no impression on our senses; because they are for the most part made up of straight lines, and I not think that any part of a line has touched our senses which was strictly straight'—and he appeals to the way straight lines look wavy under a magnifying glass. (AT, VII, 381).

These passages, it seems to me, make it likely that it is (2), and not (1), which Descartes has in mind. The theorem about the angles of a triangle is not meant to be a counterfactual about what would be the case if there were, as there are not, triangles existent in the world. It is meant to be an actual statement about something which can be a subject of predication even when there are no triangles in existence. But the question arises: in the absence of existent triangles, *what* is it that has the properties ascribed by the theorems?

Hobbes raised this question in his 14th objection. 'If a triangle exists nowhere, I do not understand how it can have a nature; for what is nowhere, is not, and therefore has not a being or a nature. . . . The truth of the proposition "a triangle is something having its three angles equal to two right angles" is everlasting. But the nature of a triangle is not everlasting; all triangles might cease to be.' Similarly, the proposition 'Man is an animal' is true forever, because names are everlasting, but when the human race ceases to be, human nature will be no more. Hobbes' objection is wrapped up in his theory that to predicate is to attach a second name to something; but it is independent of that theory. Descartes replied: 'Everybody is familiar with the distinction of essence and existence; and this talk about names as being everlasting (instead of our having notions or ideas of eternal truths) has already been sufficiently refuted.'

This reply is hardly adequate. But the following reply seems open to Descartes. What exists nowhere, neither in the world nor in thought, can have no nature, perhaps; but the triangle exists in thought, and has a true and immutable nature which persists whether or not any triangles outside thought exist or cease to be.

Let us explore that possible reply. Notice first that what has the properties which the theorems prove is not, strictly, the essence or nature of the triangle; the essence and properties belong to something, and the essence is made up of the properties which the theorems prove. But to *what* do these properties belong? What *has* the nature of a triangle whether or not any triangle exists? The text of the *Meditations* is ambiguous. '*Invenio apud me innumeras ideas quarumdam rerum, quae, etiam si extra me fortasse nullibi existant, non tamen dici possunt nihil esse; & quamvis a me quoddamodo ad arbitrium cogitentur, non tamen a me finguntur, sed suas habent veras et immutabiles naturas.*' (AT, VII, 64). Is it the *ideae*, or the *res* which have their true and immutable natures? Neither the Latin nor the French text settles it.[1] He goes on to speak of the properties which can be proved *de isto triangulo*, which seems to suggest that that to which the properties belong is a triangle. But there seems something very odd about a triangle which exists whether or not any triangle exists; and *iste triangulus* is the triangle which I imagine, so that the phrase may mean, not a triangle, but the idea of a triangle. On the other hand, we might say that the triangle of which the properties are proved is indeed a triangle but not one which exists, merely one which *datur*, which is given; *being given* to be understood as something between existence and nothingness: for it is certainly of *res*, and not of ideas, that Descartes says '*non tamen dici possunt nihil esse*'. This seems a slightly more natural way of reading the text, and accords with the *DM* which does not mention ideas. But if we read it thus, further difficulties arise.

What is the relation between the *dari* of the triangle and the occurrence of the idea of the triangle? Can we say that for the triangle, *dari est cogitari*? Or is it possible for a triangle to be given without being thought of? If it is a triangle which has an eternal and immutable nature, then it seems that *dari* cannot be identified with *cogitari*. For Descartes says 'it is not necessary for me ever to imagine any triangle; but whenever I choose to consider a rectilinear figure that has just three angles, I must ascribe to it properties from which it is rightly inferred that its three angles are not greater than two right angles'. (AT, VII, 67). Now Descartes has just said—a propos of the idea of God—that his thought imposes no necessity on things, but the necessity of the thing determines him to think (ibid., lines 5 ff.). Analogously, he should say that

[1] For *ideae*: *ad arbitrium cogitentur*: thought at will; it is ideas which are thought. For *res*: the *quae* before the colon refers to *res*; *cogitentur* would be thought *of*; natures more naturally belong to *res*. The gender is the same in both Latin and French.

this necessity of ascribing certain properties to a triangle whenever he thinks of it comes from the triangle, not from his thought. Again, we reach the conclusion that what has the eternal and immutable nature is a triangle, not the idea of a triangle; and we add to this conclusion that this triangle, which has the provable properties, *datur*, whether or not Descartes or anyone ever has an idea of a triangle. This means that we must modify what we imagined Descartes as replying to Hobbes: when Hobbes says that only what exists can have a nature, Descartes must reply that not only what exists in the world, and not only what exists in the mind, but also that which is given, whether or not it exists, has a nature.

I do not think we need to make any further distinction between the givenness of the triangle and the being of the nature of the triangle. When Descartes says '*est profecto determinata quaedam eius natura*' (AT, VII, 64, 15) I take the '*eius*' to mean 'of the triangle'; and I take it that '*est natura determinata trianguli*' means the same as '*datur triangulus determinatam habens naturam*'; the two differ, I take it, merely in being abstract and concrete ways of saying the same thing.

If I am right, we have in Descartes' apparatus three possible different states of affairs:

> triangulus datur
> triangulus cogitatur
> triangulus existit

That to which '*triangulus*' refers in each of these cases is the same, though only in the second case is there an idea of a triangle, and only in the third case is there an actually existent triangle.

Let us see if we can confirm this reading from the presentations of the ontological argument elsewhere, and from the answers to the objections. In the definitions which open the geometric proof of the existence of God in the *Second Replies*, we read: 'When we say that some attribute is contained in the nature or the concept of a thing, it is the same as if we were to say that this attribute is true of that thing'. (AT, VII, 162). The thing referred to here must be something distinct from an *existent* thing; otherwise the ontological argument based on this definition is a blatant *petitio principii*; and indeed it would be possible, by the ontological argument, to prove the existence of something corresponding to every conceivable nature.

In the *Principles* we read that when mind contemplates its ideas without affirming or denying that there is anything outside itself which corresponds to these ideas, it is beyond any danger of falling into error. As an example of the demonstrations which are possible within this field, we are given: that the three angles of a triangle are equal to two right angles. The mind, we are told, because it sees that it is necessarily involved in the idea of the triangle that it should have three angles which are equal to two right angles, is absolutely persuaded that the triangle has three angles equal to two right angles. Now the triangle which is here spoken of is not an existent triangle; for the mind is supposed to be taking care neither to affirm nor deny that anything outside itself corresponds to its ideas. Nor, it seems, is it the idea of the triangle; for the statement that the triangle has three angles equal to two right angles is presented not as a statement about the idea of the triangle, but as a conclusion which is drawn from reflection on the idea of the triangle. And this is borne out by the parallel deduction of the existence of a perfect Being. (AT, VIII, 9–10).

Perhaps the fullest working out of the ontological argument comes in the *First Answers*. (AT, VIII, 115 ff.). The kernel of the argument is stated thus: That which we clearly and distinctly understand to belong to the true and immutable nature of anything, its essence or form, can be truly affirmed of that thing. This again cannot be the existent thing, for that would involve a gross begging of the question when applied to the nature of God. This major premise is not argued for by Descartes in this place, because he says it has already been agreed by the objector that whatever we clearly and distinctly perceive is true (HR [Haldane & Ross] 2, 19). Now strictly, there is a leap here: from this principle, plus the fact that we clearly and distinctly understand some property to belong to the true and immutable nature of something, it follows only that the property in question does belong to the true and immutable nature of the thing, not that it can be truly affirmed of it. But provided we take the thing to which the property belongs to be a not necessarily existent thing, then the leap is not a big one: it involves only the further principle that what has a nature has the properties which belong to the nature. But if we take it that properties can only be affirmed of existent things, the leap is fallacious; for something might belong to the nature of triangle, and yet not be true of any triangle, because no triangle existed.

A little further on Descartes says 'If I think of a triangle ... then I shall truly affirm of the triangle all the things which I recognise to be contained in the idea of the triangle, as that its angles are equal to two right angles etc.' Once again, the triangle of which this property is truly affirmed is not any existent triangle. But what is the relation between the *nature* of the not-necessarily-existent triangle, and the *idea* of a triangle? It is not that every time I think of a triangle, I think of everything which is contained in the nature of the triangle. 'Though I can think of a triangle while restricting my thought in such a manner that I do not think at all of its three angles being equal to two right angles, yet I cannot deny that attribute of it by any clear and distinct mental operation, i.e. rightly understanding what I say'. So whatever belongs to the nature of a triangle is contained in the idea of a triangle; but not every time that I think of a triangle do I think of what is contained in the idea of a triangle. (AT, VII, 117; HR, 2, 20).

It seems to be true in general that whatever belongs to the nature of X is contained in the idea of X; but the converse is not true, that wherever we have an idea containing certain elements there is some nature composed of corresponding elements. The idea of a triangle is both simple and innate; others are composite and factitious. Some composite ideas have natures corresponding to them. Take, for instance, the idea of a triangle inscribed in a square. It is not part of the nature of a triangle to be so inscribed, nor part of the nature of a square to contain such a triangle. None the less, the composite figure itself has a true and immutable nature, and accordingly, certain properties are true of it, e.g. that the area of the square cannot be less than double that of the inscribed triangle. But others do not. The idea, for instance, of a Hippogriff or winged horse is a composite and factitious idea. (AT, VII, 37). This comes out in the control which the mind has over such ideas. 'Those ideas which do not contain a true and immutable nature, but only a fictitious one put together by the mind, can be divided by the same mind, not merely by abstraction or restriction of thought but by a clear and distinct operation.' What mind has put together, mind can put asunder. 'For example, when I think of a winged horse ... I easily understand that I can on the contrary think of a horse without wings'—not just think of a horse without thinking of his wings, but think of a horse without wings, clearly understanding what I'm talking about. So here we have an idea which contains the property of being winged, plus the properties constituting the nature of horse; but there is no thing, existent or non-existent, which has these properties as its nature. (AT, VII, 117).

I do not think that Descartes makes clear what is supposed to be the difference between the winged horse and the triangle inscribed in the square. If I can think of a horse without wings, equally I can think of a triangle not inscribed in a square. If I cannot think of a triangle-in-a-square without certain properties, equally I cannot think of a winged horse without wings. Perhaps the difference is this. The properties of a winged horse are just the sum total of the properties of a horse and the properties of being winged. But the proportion which Descartes mentions as a property of a triangle inscribed in a square is not a property of a triangle as such, considered without reference to any square; nor is it a property of a square as such, considered without reference to any triangle. 'I cannot think of a winged horse without wings' is true because I cannot think of a winged X without wings, no matter what X may be. 'I cannot think of a triangle inscribed in an X which is more than half the area of the figure in which it is inscribed' is not true no matter what X may be.

Descartes' views as I have expounded them bear a strong resemblance to those of Meinong. Just as Descartes distinguishes between '*datur*' and '*existere*' so Meinong makes a distinction between '*es gibt*' and '*sein*'. For Descartes not only what exists has a nature but also what is given has a nature. Similarly, Meinong writes 'The figures with which geometry is concerned do not exist. Nevertheless their properties can be established'. He called this the principle of the independence of *Sosein* from *Sein*. For Descartes it is not necessary that there should be an idea of X for a non-existent X to be given and have properties. Similarly, Meinong wrote 'it is no more necessary to an object that it be presented [to the mind] in order not to exist than it is in order for it to exist'. For Descartes there is something which is a triangle whether or not any triangle exists. Such a triangle is surely very like a Meinongian Pure Object, which 'stands beyond being and non-being'.[2]

---

[2] See Meinong's Theory of Objects, translated in Roderick M. Chisholm (ed.), *Realism and the Background of Phenomenology*, (Glencoe, 1960), 76 ff. The passage quoted are from pp. 82, 83, 86 respectively.

Within the realm of being, Meinong makes a further distinction between subsistence (*Bestand*) and existence (*Existenz*). He gives as examples of things which subsist: similarities, differences, numbers, logical connections, or the existence of the antipodes. If two objects are similar, then there subsists a similarity between them. Roughly, subsistence appears to be the being of abstract objects, and existence appears to be the being of concrete objects. The corresponding distinction in Descartes would seem to be that between two sorts of being or *entitas*, namely modal being (*entitas modalis*), which belongs to the attributes of things, and reality (*realitas*) which belongs only to substances. 'Whatever is real can exist separately from any other subject; and whatever can exist thus separately is a substance' (VII, 434; cf. AT, III, 430; VII, 253, 364).

II

So far we have been considering the first stage of Descartes' ontological argument, his statement that 'assuming a triangle, its three angles must be equal to two right angles'. We must now turn to his application of his principles. 'Going back to an examination of my idea of a perfect Being, I found that this included the existence of such a being. Consequently ... it is ... certain that God, the perfect being in question, is or exists'. So the *Discourse*, arguing from the idea of God. The *Meditations* reaches the same conclusion from a consideration of the essence of God. 'I clearly see that existence can no more be separated from the essence of God than can its having three angles equal to two right angles be separated from the essence of a triangle, or the idea of a mountain from the idea of a valley; and so there is no less absurdity in thinking of a God (a supremely perfect being) who lacks existence than in thinking of a mountain without a valley.' (AT, VII, 66).

Gassendi, anticipating Kant, objected that existence should not be compared in this manner with a property. 'Neither in God nor in anything else is existence a perfection, but rather that without which there are no perfections. . . . Existence can't be said to exist in a thing like a perfection; and if a thing lacks existence, then it is not just imperfect or lacking perfection; it is nothing at all. When you were listing the perfections of a triangle, you did not count existence, and you did not draw any conclusion about the existence of the triangle. Similarly, when listing the perfections of God, you should not have included existence, or drawn the conclusion that God exists, unless you want to beg the question.' (AT VII, 323).

Descartes replied: 'I do not see what sort of thing you want existence to be, nor why it can't be called a property just as much as omnipotence, provided that we use the word 'property' for any attribute, or whatever can be predicated of a thing'. (VII, 382). Fairly clearly, he had missed the point of Gassendi's criticism, but equally, Gassendi's remarks were based in their turn on a misunderstanding. He did not realise that for Descartes, the subject of the sentence 'God exists' was a pure object, beyond being and non-being. A pure object can have properties whether or not it exists; but if we are inquiring about its properties, one of the most interesting questions we can ask is 'does it exist or not?' In making predications of a pure object we are not begging the question of its existence; and when Descartes concludes 'God exists' from the premise 'God is supremely perfect' he is drawing his conclusion not from the occurrence of the word 'God' in the subject-place of his premiss, but because he believes the predicate 'exists' is included in the predicate 'is supremely perfect'. The objection 'existence is not a predicate' amounts to this: 'exists' cannot be a predicate because if it is false of any subject then there is no such subject for it to be false of. But this objection has no force unless there is an independent argument to show that Meinongian pure objects are incoherent. For even if there is no God, so that 'God exists' is false, there is always the appropriate pure object to sustain the false predicate.

Hume denied that existence could form part of the content of an idea. 'The idea of existence is nothing different from the idea of any object, and when after the simple conception of any thing we would conceive it as existent, we in reality make no addition or alteration on our first idea.' (*Treatise*, I, III, 7). The idea of an existent X is the same as the idea of an X. Descartes to some extent anticipated this line of objection. 'We never think of things without thinking of them as existents' he wrote (AT, VIII, 117). All ideas, therefore, in a sense contain existence. (AT, VII, 166). But whereas the ideas of other things contain possible existence, the idea of God contains necessary existence. The mind sees that in the idea of a supremely perfect being, 'there is contained existence—not merely possible and contingent existence, as in the ideas of all other things which it distinctly perceives, but altogether necessary and eternal existence.' (AT, VII, 116, VIII, 10).

Descartes' meaning seems to be this. Take the defining properties of any entity; let 'F' represent a predicate-term for those properties. If we can clearly and distinctly conceive of an entity which is F, then we know that it is *possible* for an entity which is F to exist. In the case of God, however, we can draw a stronger conclusion. Where the properties in question are those which define God, we know that it is *necessary* for an entity which is F to exist. 'We conceive clearly that actual existence is necessarily and always conjoint with the other attributes of God.' (AT, VII, 116).

This is proved by Descartes in two distinct manners. Commonly, he argues that since God is perfect, and existence is a perfection, it follows necessarily that God exists (AT, VII, 66; 166; also *DM*). In the *First Replies*, it is not from God's perfection, but from His omnipotence that the argument is drawn. 'Because we cannot think of God's existence as being possible, without at the same time, and by taking heed of His immeasurable power, acknowledging that He can exist by His own might, we hence conclude that He really exists and has existed from all eternity; for the light of nature makes it most plain that what can exist by its own power always exists'. (AT, VII, 119).

This last passage creates a peculiar mental discomfort; at least, we feel, there must be some important premises suppressed. Descartes himself was not altogether happy about the argument. At first he had written thus: 'We cannot think of His existence as being possible without at the same time thinking that it must be possible for there to be some power by means of which He exists; and that power cannot be conceived to be in anything else than in that same supremely powerful being; and so we conclude that He can exist by His own might.' But before these words went to the printer, he asked Mersenne to cancel them so that the curious could not decipher them, in case anybody attacked the author 'in the place which he himself judged to be the weakest.' (AT, III, 330).

The stages of the argument seem to be as follows.
(1) God's existence is possible.
This is shown because we have a clear and distinct idea of God (AT, VII, 119); and this in turn is proved because 'whatever I clearly and distinctly perceive, which is real and true and involves some perfection is all contained in [the idea of God]' (AT, VII, 46). (Cf. VII, 150). This is the part of the argument which Leibniz thought deficient. It needed to be proved, he said, that all perfections were compatible with each other; otherwise the idea of an all-perfect being would imply a contradiction. Leibniz himself was prepared to offer such a proof, which convinced Spinoza but has not satisfied modern critics.³

(2) God is by definition all-powerful and independent. This is said in the third Meditation (VII, 45, etc.). It followed from this, Descartes thought, that if He can exist at all He can exist by his own power. But we know that God can exist. Therefore:
(3) God can exist by his own power.
(4) What can exist by its own power, does exist.
It is this step which at first sight seems most in need of justification. I suggest that there are two suppressed premisses. (a) If you can do something by your own power, and you do not do it, then it can only be because you do not want to do it; (b) everything wants to exist. Now (a) is plausible enough, and is commonly accepted when it is appealed to in a famous formulation of the Problem of Evil ('If God can prevent evils, and does not prevent them, then he must not want to prevent them'). (b) sounds odd to us, but in fact *omnia appetunt esse* was a scholastic commonplace. Now (a) and (b) together yield (4), and (3) and (4) together give
(5) God exists.

One misgiving which we may feel here concerns the application of (b) to Pure Objects. We may be prepared to go so far with Descartes and Meinong as to admit that non-existent entities can have natures and properties, but surely they cannot have *desires*? This misgiving seems unfounded. If we are to make predications of the non-existent at all, among the predications we must make will be some which involve desires. For instance, we shall have to say that centaurs (though no centaurs exist) have the libidinous appetites ascribed to them by classical authorities. A non-libidinous centaur would not be a centaur at all.

³ It is, however, accepted by Russell: *Philosophy of Leibniz*, 174.

The premises from which Descartes here derives the existence of God have always been true; therefore he concludes not only that God exists, but that he has existed from all eternity. 'For the light of nature makes it most plain that what can exist by its own power always exists.'

The light of nature can do so, I contend, only if it shows us also that everything desires existence. '*Omnia appetunt esse*' is explicitly supplied by Aquinas as a suppressed premiss to rescue from fallacy an argument of Aristotle's which purported to show that whatever can corrupt sometimes does corrupt, so that any everlasting being must be a necessary being.[4] Now when scholastics spoke of 'necessary being' they did not mean a being whose existence was a necessary truth; they meant a being which, in the order of nature, could not cease to exist. For medieval Aristotelians the stars were necessary beings in this sense. Their existence was not a necessary truth; it was contingent on the will of God, who might never have created. But they were naturally indestructible, and could cease to exist only by being annihilated by their creator. Obviously, something whose existence was a logically necessary truth, would *a fortiori* be necessary in the scholastic sense; but the converse does not hold.

It is important to underline this distinction. A recent revival of the Ontological Argument runs as follows: 'If God, a being greater than which cannot be conceived, does not exist, then He cannot come into existence. . . . Since He cannot come into existence, if He does not exist His existence is impossible. If He does exist, He cannot have come into existence . . . nor can He cease to exist, for nothing could cause Him to cease to exist nor could it just happen that He ceased to exist. So if God exists, His existence is necessary. Thus God's existence is either impossible or necessary. It can be the former only if the concept of such a being is self-contradictory or in some way logically absurd. Assuming that this is not so, it follows that He necessarily exists'.[5]

In this argument there is a fallacy: 'impossible' is being used in two senses, in one of which it is contrasted with the modern notion of logical necessity, in the other of which it is contrasted with the medieval notion of necessary being. In the first sense it

[4] Cf. C. J. F. Williams, Aristotle and Corruptibility, *Religious Studies*, 1, 19, who quotes Aquinas *in lib.* I *de Caelo et Mundo, lectio* xxvi, n. 6.
[5] Malcolm, 'Anselm's Ontological Argument', *Philosophical Review*, 49, p. 48.

means 'involving the violation of a logical truth' in the second it means 'incapable of being brought into or put out of existence'. The statement 'If God does not exist His existence is impossible' may be true in the sense that if God does not exist he cannot be brought into existence, without being true in the sense that if God does not exist, the statement 'God exists' must involve the violation of a logical truth. But it must be true in the latter sense if the argument is to work.

Now it might seem that an analogous fallacy is being committed by Descartes when he argues that if God can exist at all, He can exist by his own power. For does not the first 'can' refer to logical possibility, whereas the second 'can' relates to powers residing in natural agents? I think, in fact, Descartes' argument does not contain this fallacy, though it moves rather too fast. Premise (1) above certainly only shows that it is logically possible for God to exist, not that God has any power to exist. That God has the power to exist follows not from premiss (1), but from the different premiss that God is all-powerful: he can do everything, including exist. That God can exist *by his own power* follows from this plus the premiss that God is independent, i.e. that he can do whatever he can do without help from anything else. That this is the line of Descartes' thought is I think shown by the passage which he ordered Mersenne to cancel, though we may well sympathise with his despairing of presenting it in a clear and plausible manner.

Certainly, Descartes was aware of the possibility of the fallacious argument recorded above, and he pointed out the fallacy. In the *Second Replies* he discusses the argument 'If it is not self-contradictory for God to exist, then it is certain that he exists; but it is not self-contradictory for him to exist; *ergo* . . .' This argument, he says, is a sophism. 'For in the major the word 'self-contradictory' has reference to the concept of a cause from which God would derive existence; in the minor, however, it refers only to the concept of the divine existence and nature. This is clear from the following. If the major is denied, it is proved as follows: if God does not yet exist, it is self-contradictory for him to exist, because there cannot be any cause sufficient to produce Him; but it is not self-contradictory for him to exist, *ergo* . . . But if the minor is denied, we shall have to say that is not self-contradictory, in the formal concept of which there is nothing which involves a contradiction; but in the formal concept of the divine existence or nature there is nothing which involves a contradiction, *ergo*. . . . And these two are very different.' Descartes' God exists necessarily, in the sense that 'God exists' is a necessary truth.

It seems to me that if we give Descartes his Meinongian assumptions, there is nothing fallacious in his argument. This makes it the more extraordinary that Meinong himself did not accept the ontological argument. When he said that objects as such were beyond being and not being, Meinong was careful to add qualifications. 'This is not to say, of course, that an Object can neither be nor not be. Nor is it to say that the question, whether or not the Object has being, is purely accidental to the nature of every Object. An absurd Object such as a round square carries in itself the guarantee of its own non-being in every sense; an ideal Object, such as diversity, carries in itself the guarantee of its own non-existence'. If this is so, one might ask Meinong, why cannot there be an Object which carries in itself the guarantee of its own existence?

Russell, reviewing Meinong in *Mind* 1905 (p. 533) claimed that he could not in consistency reject the ontological proof. 'If the round square is round and square the existent round square is existent and round and square. Thus something round and square exists although everything round and square is impossible. This ontological argument cannot be avoided by Kant's device of saying that existence is not a predicate. For [the Meinongians] admit that "existing" applies when and only when being "actual" applies, and that the latter is a *sosein*. Thus we cannot escape the consequence that the "existent God" both exists and is God, and it is hard to see how it can be maintained. . . that this has no bearing on the question whether God exists.' Meinong could only reply that though God was existent, to be existent and to exist were not the same. Russell was surely right to be dissatisfied with such a reply.

Descartes, more consistent than Meinong, accepted the ontological argument; more cautious than Meinong, he is not vulnerable to Russell's argument about the round square. It is customary to dismiss Meinongian pure objects with a highhanded reference to their 'oddity', or by an appeal for 'a robust sense of reality'. Descartes would have regarded such a feeling for reality as a mere prejudice. More serious are the objections that such objects involve violations of the principle of non-contradiction. The round square, for instance, is both square (by definition) and not square (since whatever is round is not square). Descartes could reply that this contradiction was the result, not of admitting pure objects, but of admitting impossible entities among them. Though Meinong did this, Descartes never did. He wrote: in the concept of every thing there is contained either possible or necessary existence; (AT, VIII, 2a, 60); what cannot exist therefore is no thing. 'Possible existence' he wrote 'is a perfection in the idea of a triangle, just as necessary existence is a perfection in the idea of God; it is this which makes it superior to the ideas of those chimaeras whose existence is regarded as nil' (*nulla*). (AT, VIII, 383). He would not have been trapped by the argument that if a round circle is impossible, then there must *be* something (viz. the round circle) to be impossible. 'All self-contradiction (*implicantia*) or impossibility' he wrote 'arises in our conception, which mistakenly joins together ideas which clash with each other. It cannot be situated in anything outside the mind, because if something is outside the mind, then *eo ipso* it is not self-contradictory, but possible.' (AT, VII, 152).

Descartes has an answer, too, to another argument suggested by Russell, namely, that if existence is a predicate, then we can conceive an existent golden mountain, and this must in its turn exist. He appeals to the distinction between true and immutable essences on the one hand, and fictitious essences on the other. If F is part of the true and immutable essence of G it is impossible for us to conceive of a G which is not F. If, on the other hand, we can conceive of a G which is not F, then even though we can make up the notion of a G which is F, this will be a fictional essence and not an immutable essence. 'For example, when I think of a winged horse, or of a lion actually existing, or of a triangle inscribed in a square, I easily understand that I can on the contrary think of a horse without wings, of a lion as not existing and of a triangle apart from a square, and so forth, and that hence these things have no true and immutable essence.' An existent golden mountain, then, does not have a true and immutable essence, and therefore no conclusion can be drawn about its existence. God, unlike the existent golden mountain, is no fiction, because we can prove *a priori* that what has the properties of God has also existence though we cannot prove *a priori* that what has the properties of a golden mountain has also existence. None the less, if Descartes is to avoid the conclusion that the existent golden mountain exists, it seems that he must deny that there is any such thing as the existent golden mountain: he must exclude it from the realm of pure objects. I do not know of any place where he explicitly does so; but it is compatible with all the texts known to me. In conclusion, we may say that Descartes' argument is most intelligible if we regard him as admitting, with Meinong, that there is a status of pure objecthood, beyond being and not-being, but, unlike Meinong, denying this status to impossible and fictional entities, and restricting it to those entities which have true and immutable essences, i.e. those about which non-trivial truths can be proved *a priori*.

The most serious—indeed the insurmountable—objection to Meinongian pure objects is that it is impossible to provide any criterion of identity for them. If something is to be a subject of which we can make predications, it is essential that it shall be possible to tell in what circumstances two predications are made of *that same subject*. Otherwise we shall never be able to apply e.g. the principle that contradictory predications may not be made of the same subject. We have various complicated criteria by which we decide whether two statements are being made about the same actual man; by what criteria can we decide whether two statements are being made about the same *possible* man? The difficulties are entertainingly brought out in a famous passage in Quine's *On What there Is*.

> Take, for instance, the possible fat man in that doorway; and again, the possible bald man in that doorway. Are they the same possible man, or two possible men? How do we decide? How many possible men are there in that doorway? Are there more possible thin ones than fat ones? How many of them are alike? Or would their being alike make them one? Are no *two* possible things alike? Is this the same as saying that it is impossible for two things to be alike? Or, finally, is the concept of identity simply inapplicable to unactualised possibles? But what sense can be found in talking of entities which cannot meaningfully be said to be identical with themselves and distinct from one another?

These objections are, I think, ultimately insurmountable and make untenable the notion of Meinongian pure objects: we may with gratitude accept the alternative method of dealing with the non-existent offered, with the aid of quantifiers, by Frege and Russell. But it is perhaps worth remarking that when the pure object in question is God, then the difficulties about identification appear less palpable. For, in the nature of the case, only one omnipotent and all-perfect being is possible; so that we do not feel constrained to put to Descartes the question '*Which* God are you proving the existence of?'

I shall not pursue these difficulties further in this paper, but I wish to conclude by drawing attention to a major difficulty internal to Descartes' own system. If the ontological argument is not to be a great *petitio principii*, it is essential that it should be possible to prove properties of the problematically existent. It must be possible, at least in some cases, to be sure that X is F without being sure that X exists. But if that is so, then what becomes of the *cogito ergo sum*? It is an essential step in the *cogito* that every attribute must belong to a substance. '*Pour penser il faut être*,' he says several times, is a necessary presupposition if the *cogito* is to work. And this is a particular example of a general principle, stated in the fifth definition of the *more geometrico* proof, and stated thus in *Principles of Philosophy* 1, II. 'It is very manifest by the natural light which is in our souls, that no qualities or properties pertain to nothing; and that where some are perceived there must necessarily be some thing or substance on which they depend.' But what right has Descartes to assume that the substance in question exists? If I can be sure that a triangle has its angles equal to three right angles without being sure that any triangle exists, why can I not be sure that *ego cogito* without being sure that *ego existo*? On the other hand, if I can argue 'I think, therefore, I am', why can I not argue 'The triangle has three angles equal to two right angles, therefore the triangle exists?'

Perhaps I was incautious in saying that '*pour penser il faut être*' is a particular example of the principle of natural light. For what that principle shows us is that attributes cannot be attributes of *nothing*. But 'not to be nothing' and 'to exist' are not synonyms: does not Descartes speak of the ideas of 'things which even if they perhaps exist nowhere outside myself, cannot be said to be nothing?' (AT, VII, 63). But if I was incautious, so is Descartes. In the exposition of the *cogito* in the *Meditations* itself, he trades on the two being equivalent: the deceiver 'nunquam efficiet *ut nihil sim* quamdiu me aliquid esse cogitabo'; and straightway he concludes to the truth of '*ego existo*'. (AT, VII, 25).

Descartes says that his system rests on two principles: His own existence and God's existence. If my account is right he cannot have both these principles in quite the way he wants them. If what does not exist can have properties, then he can perhaps prove God's existence, but he cannot prove his own. If what does not exist cannot have properties, he can perhaps prove his own existence, but he cannot prove God's existence by the ontological argument. The *cogito* and the ontological argument cannot both be valid.

Descartes' Ontological Proof

NORMAN MALCOLM

I

Descartes' statement that when he imagines or assumes a triangle certain properties can be demonstrated of this triangle (*de isto triangulo*) even if no triangle exists in the world or outside of his thought, perplexes Mr. Kenny. He wonders *what it is* that has those properties. He thinks it cannot be the *idea* of a triangle, nor can it be an existent triangle. He speculates over a possible distinction between a triangle's being *given* and its being *thought of*. He concludes that a triangle might be *given* even if no one ever thought of a triangle. He also concludes that what Descartes was referring to, when he imagined a triangle, was a 'pure object' which is 'beyond being and non-being'. In Descartes' ontological proof the subject of the sentence 'God exists' (Kenny supposes) was also a pure object. Kenny defends pure objects against some criticisms, but holds that there is an 'insurmountable' objection to them, viz., that there cannot be any criterion of identity for them.

Let me say, first, that Kenny has not made me understand what it is for something to be *given* without being *thought of*. I shall say nothing more about this alleged distinction. Second, I think it would be advisable to amplify our understanding of how Descartes uses the word 'idea'. Third, I believe that what basically puzzles Kenny is the notion of *an object of thought*, a notion that is a perpetual source of philosophical confusion. Fourth, I will make a suggestion about the importance, for Descartes, of the distinction between 'mental fictions' and 'true and immutable natures'. Finally, I address myself briefly to the supposed mistake of reasoning that Kenny attributes to me.

II

To turn to Descartes' use of the word 'idea': he himself says that it is ambiguous, sometimes meaning 'an act of my understanding', sometimes meaning 'the thing which is represented by this act.'[1] He also says that an idea is an image or picture. 'The ideas in me are like pictures or images...'(HR I, 163: AT VII, 42). Descartes uses the word 'thought' (*cogitatio*) in a very broad sense. Feeling fear and feeling pain would be thoughts (or thinking): so would be willing, approving, affirming, denying, and so on. He says:
> Some of these [thoughts of mine] are, as it were, images of things; the name of idea belongs properly to those alone: as when I think [of] a man, or a chimaera, or heaven, or an angel, or God. But other [thoughts of mine] have certain other forms besides: as when I will, when I fear, when I affirm, when I deny, I do indeed always apprehend some thing as the object of my thought, but in the thought I comprehend something still more than the similitude of that thing; and some of these [thoughts of mine] are called volitions, or affections, and others judgments' (HR, I, 159: AT, VII, 37).[2]

I understand Descartes to be holding that every operation of the mind (e.g. feeling, or sensing, or judging) contains a picture, likeness or representation (that is, an *idea*) of something. That which is represented is the object of the (act of) thought. One's thought has an object regardless of whether anything in the world corresponds to it. Towards the object of a particular thought one takes up some attitude, such as desiring it, or willing it, or fearing it, or judging that it corresponds to reality. A representation of something is contained in every mental operation.

When Descartes speaks of 'the objective reality of an idea' we must remember his double use of the word 'idea', to mean either

---

[1] *Descartes' Philosophical Works*, edited by Haldane and Ross, vol. I, 138: *Oeuvres de Descartes*, edited by Adam and Tannery, vol. VII, 8.
[2] I am indebted to Professor Norman Kretzmann for the translation of this passage and also for helpful suggestions as to its interpretation.

an act of thinking, or what is represented by (or in) an act of thinking. In the phrase, 'the objective reality of an idea', the word 'idea' means an act of thinking; and 'the objective reality' of the act of thinking is the object of the act, i.e. what is represented. Descartes is using the word 'idea' in the sense of the object of an act of thinking when he says that 'an idea is the thing thought of itself, in so far as it is objectively in the understanding' (HR, II, 9: AT, IX, 81). In this sense 'the idea of the sun will be the sun itself existing in the mind. . . ' (HR, II, 10: AT, IX, 82). I can think of the sun whether or not the sun exists. The object of my thought is *the sun*—nothing less. I can think of my paternal grandmother, who no longer exists. The object of my thought is my grandmother herself—not some other thing—not, for example, a mental image of her. I can think of a triangle, and demonstrate properties of it, whether or not a triangle exists. I can think of God, and ascribe properties to Him, whether or not He exists.

III

Kenny wonders *what it is* that has the properties or the nature of a triangle even if no triangle exists. He remarks how Descartes speaks of the properties which can be proved *de isto triangulo*. To Kenny this 'seems to suggest that that to which the properties belong is a triangle. But there seems something very odd about a triangle which exists "whether or not any triangle exists" (Kenny, p. 6). But who said anything about a triangle *which exists* whether or not any triangle exists? Descartes is thinking about a triangle, and what he is thinking about (a triangle) has essential properties from which he can demonstrate other properties. Descartes (and you and I) can do this regardless of whether there are any triangles. I suspect that Kenny has made the error of assuming that if one is thinking of a triangle, one must be thinking of a triangle *that exists*.

If there are no triangles, is it the *idea* of a triangle, rather than a triangle, that has the nature of a triangle? The answer depends on which of the two senses of 'idea' one has in mind. The idea of a triangle, in the sense of an act of thinking of a triangle, certainly does not have the nature of a triangle. The idea of a triangle, in the sense of *the object* of an act of thinking of a triangle, *does* have the nature of a triangle. It *is* a triangle! But we must avoid the assumption that the proposition 'He is thinking of a triangle' entails the proposition 'There exists a triangle of which he is thinking'.

Are objects of thought 'beyond being and non-being'? Perhaps so, if one means that merely from the fact that something is an object of thought it cannot be determined whether it exists or not. But that exotic mode of expression should be avoided: for it suggests that objects of thought as such have an ineffable kind of existence, different from any run-of-the-mill kind of existence. Speaking of 'intentional objects' (of which objects of thought would be one category) Miss Anscombe remarks that we should not think 'there is any sense in questions as to the kind of existence —the ontological status—of intentional objects as such. All such questions are senseless.'[3] I agree. Suppose a philosopher asks: 'Assuming there are no triangles, what kind of being does the triangle have of which I am thinking?' What can one make of such a question? He is thinking of *a triangle*. What else is there to say?

In discussing the ontological proof Kenny makes a curious mistake. He cites Descartes' statement that 'To say that some attribute is contained in the nature or the concept of a thing is the same as to say that this attribute is true of that thing' (HR, II, 57: AT, VII, 162). Kenny offers the following comment: 'The thing referred to here must be something distinct from an *existent* thing; otherwise the ontological argument based on this definition is a blatant *petitio principii*' (Kenny, p.22 ; cf. p. 23). Later on Kenny says that 'for Descartes, the subject of the sentence "God exists" was a pure object, beyond being and non-being' (p. 27). Now this second remark results in absurdity. For if Descartes meant the subject of the sentence 'God exists' to be something that is 'beyond being', then he could not use the sentence to assert that God exists!

The only precaution Descartes must take to avoid *petitio principii* is to avoid *assuming* that God exists. But of course he does not have to, and cannot, assume that God does *not* exist. He cannot use the word 'God' to refer to 'something distinct from an *existent* thing', as Kenny says he must. All he has to do is to make God an object of thought, without assuming either that God exists or that God does not exist.

[3] G. E. M. Anscombe, 'The Intentionality of Sensation', *Analytical Philosophy*, Second Series, edited by R. J. Butler, Oxford, 1965, p. 168.

I see no merit in Kenny's claim that it is impossible to provide criteria of identity for objects of thought. His claim is actually made about so-called 'Meinongian pure objects', but it is relevant to Descartes only if it applies to objects of thought. Descartes correctly assumes that he can think of a triangle whether or not any triangle exists, and that he can think of a supremely perfect being whether or not such a being exists. If I am thinking of an equilateral triangle and you are thinking of a right-angled one, then we are not thinking of the same triangle. If we are both thinking of a right-angled triangle, but you stipulate that yours has a hypotenuse of a certain length and I specify that the hypotenuse of mine is of a different length, then to that extent we are not thinking of the same triangle. If you are thinking of something, x, and I am thinking of something, y, and we agree to stipulate the same and only the same properties, F, for x and y, then x and y are the same object of thought. The answer to Quine's question as to whether the concept of identity applies to 'unactualized possibles' is in the affirmative. If I imagine a fat man standing in that doorway and you imagine a thin man standing in the same doorway, then we are not imagining the same man. The identity or difference is decided by considering the descriptions by which we designate the objects we are imagining. Thus what Kenny thinks is an 'insurmountable objection' to the notion of objects of thought that may or may not exist is no objection at all.

IV

A hard point to understand in Descartes' ontological proof is his distinction between a 'mental fiction' and 'a true and immutable nature'. He thinks that the failure to see this distinction results in a failure to grasp the significance of the ontological proof:

> Because we do not distinguish that which belongs to the true and immutable nature of a thing from that which we by a mental fiction assign to it, even if we do fairly clearly perceive that existence belongs to God's essence, we nevertheless do not conclude that God exists, because we do not know whether His essence is true and immutable or only a fiction we invent (HR, II, 19: AT, IX, 92).

The doctrine of true and immutable natures is identical, I believe, with the doctrine of 'simple natures' that he expounds in the

Regulae. In Rule XII he declares that the simple natures are completely known through themselves and are indefinable (HR I, 46: AT, X, 426). Furthermore, 'no knowledge is at any time possible of anything beyond those simple natures and what may be called their intermixture or combination with each other' (HR I, 43: AT, X, 422). Descartes was, like Leibniz, and Wittgenstein of the *Tractatus*, a logical atomist. Some examples he gives of simple natures are extension, figure, motion, duration, number, existence, thought, doubt.

Descartes held this doctrine throughout his life. In a letter to Princess Elizabeth in 1643, he says that 'there are in us certain primitive notions—the originals, so to say, on the pattern of which we form all other knowledge'.[4] He remarks that 'all human knowledge consists just in properly distinguishing these notions and attaching each of them only to the objects that it applies to' (Ibid, p. 276: AT, III, 665).

The idea of a supremely perfect being is one of the simple natures. In Meditation III he argues pointedly that this object of thought cannot be derived from sense-perception, nor can it be a product of human composition.

Why did Descartes think it important to understand the difference between simple (true and immutable) natures and mental fictions, in order to appreciate the ontological proof? I suggest the following explanation: In Rule XII he declares that some simple natures are joined to one another by *necessary* connections. For example, figure is necessarily united with extension, and motion is necessarily joined with duration. 'It is impossible to conceive of a figure that has no extension, nor of a motion that has no duration' (HR, I, 42: AT, X, 421). Now if A and B are both *simple* (i.e., non-composite) and if A and B are necessarily connected, this necessary connection cannot be analytic (in Kant's sense) but must be synthetic. The ontological proof reveals a necessary connection between the notion of a supremely perfect being and the notion of existence. If one believed that the notion of a supremely perfect being was a mental fiction, something *put together by us*, he would probably think that one of the elements out of which we constructed it was the notion of existence. Thus he would think that the proposition that a supremely perfect being exists is true, *but*

[4] *Descartes: Philosophical Writings*, edited by Anscombe and Geach, Nelson, 1954, p. 275: AT III, 665).

trivial, by virtue of being merely analytic. He would think that it says *nothing about reality*, but merely unpacks our own intellectual construction. Once he understands, however, that the concept of a supremely perfect being is a simple concept, not compounded by us out of other concepts, he will also realize that the ontological proof reveals a *synthetic* (although *necessary*) truth about reality. He will see that the concept of existence is *not* a definitional component of the concept of a perfect being.

V

I will comment briefly on the supposed fallacy that Kenny attributes to me. I was trying to expound the reasoning of St. Anselm of Canterbury.[5] If my exposition was correct, and if Kenny is right, then Anselm committed the same fallacy. The fallacy is supposed to consist in confusing 'the modern notion of logical necessity' with 'the medieval notion of necessary being' (Kenny, pp. 30–31). Kenny says that 'when scholastics spoke of "necessary being" they did not mean a being whose existence was a necessary truth; they meant a being which, in the order of nature, could not cease to exist' (Kenny, p. 30).

I suppose that Anselm was a 'scholastic'. But certainly he held that God is (in Kenny's phrase) 'a being whose existence is a necessary truth'. I will reproduce a succinct argument of Anselm's which contains the fallacy, if it is one, to which Kenny objects. First, Anselm states that God (characterized as 'that than which a greater cannot be conceived') cannot be conceived to exist save as without a beginning (*non potest cogitari esse nisi sine initio*).[6] This seemed obvious to Anselm. If anyone doubts that it is so, let him consider that if some being were to come into existence, there would be a cause of its coming into existence, and therefore this being would have been dependent for its coming into existence on something other than itself. Since God is conceived as an absolutely independent being, He cannot be conceived to come into existence, i.e. to begin to exist.

Anselm's argument continues: Whatever can be conceived to exist but does not exist, can be conceived to begin to exist (*per*

---

[5] Norman Malcolm, 'Anselm's Ontological Arguments', *Knowledge and Certainty*, Englewood Cliffs, 1963.
[6] *Reply to Gaunilo* 1; *St. Anselm's Proslogion*, edited by M. J. Charlesworth, Oxford, 1965, p. 168.

initium potest cogitari esse).[7] Consequently, God cannot be conceived to exist and yet not exist. If, therefore, God can be conceived to exist, He exists of necessity (*ex necessitate est*).[8]

Notice that the conclusion of this argument is a conditional proposition: *If* God can be conceived to exist He exists of necessity. In other words, *either* God cannot be conceived to exist, *or* He exists of necessity. I see no fallacy or sophism in Anselm's argument. Both Kenny and Descartes may have failed to note that it is a property of 'the formal concept of the divine nature' (Kenny, p. 32) that God cannot *come into existence* and, therefore, if He does not exist it is logically impossible that He should exist. I believe that Anselm correctly presents us with the following alternatives: Either God is not a conceivable being, or else it is a necessary truth that God exists. The point could be stated like this: The only possible explanation of the non-existence of God would be a contradiction or incoherence in our concept of God.

TERENCE PENELHUM

If I may risk summarising Mr. Kenny's examination of Descartes' variants on the Ontological Argument, I interpret him as holding that, contrary to common opinion, they have to be regarded as valid if we grant Descartes a fundamental assumption. This is the assumption that God may be regarded as possessing Meinongian being, or pure objecthood. To say of something that it has pure objecthood is to say it has a mode of being sufficient for it to be the bearer of a nature or essence, so that it can have at least some predicates ascribed to it in a non-hypothetical manner; yet it is not to say that it exists in the world. So in at least some cases existence-in-the-world need not be presupposed in the ascription of a predicate to a thing, and has to be established independently. It may not be established at all. In other words, it is quite possible that we may correctly ascribe some predicates to a pure subject that turns out on examination not to have real existence. One example of this is a (or rather *the*) triangle, which has an essence which enables us to learn of it that it has interior angles equal to

[7] Ibid., p. 170.
[8] Ibid.

180 degrees, when we know quite well that the world contains no genuine triangles. In the case of God, Descartes argues, on Mr. Kenny's reading of him, we can (uniquely) establish his real existence by gaining a deeper understanding of the essence he has. This understanding, however, is not presupposed in the initial recognition that there is a divine essence for us to contemplate; all that is necessary for this is divine pure objecthood.

Descartes, as Kenny interprets him, refines this assumption in one important way. Pure objecthood belongs only to certain entities and not to others. It belongs only to those entities about which we can demonstrate a priori truths of a non-trivial sort. The only clear non-divine examples of this class of entities are mathematical objects.

Given this assumption, Kenny argues, Descartes can avoid one obvious difficulty in the Ontological Argument. Its critics say that in order to ascribe perfections to God, the user of the argument must first assume him to exist in reality; so a subsequent deduction of his real existence is only made possible by begging the question at the outset. Descartes can avoid this criticism since, given our assumption, he only needs to begin by ascribing pure objecthood to God, and can subsequently deduce his real existence from the perfections he is then able to attribute to him. In particular, Kenny argues that given the assumption, the following two arguments (which I paraphrase) are sound:

I. God has all perfections
    Existence is a perfection.
so God exists.
II. Anything that God does not do he does not do because he does not want to do it
    God wants to exist.
so God exists.

What are we to make of the assumption? Kenny suggests two reasons for questioning it. One is a domestic, Cartesian difficulty: if the ascription of a predicate *a priori* to a subject does not entail the subject's real existence, the *cogito* fails. The other is more general: it does not seem possible to supply criteria of identity for pure objects. This latter difficulty, however, Kenny suggests may be lessened by the uniqueness of God. I think he himself would subscribe to the view he reads into Descartes, that any objection based on an appeal to a 'robust sense of reality' would be a mere expression of prejudice.

I

I shall assume throughout that Kenny's exegesis of Descartes is correct. I shall not comment on his internal criticism of Descartes. Nor shall I pursue the suggestion that God's uniqueness may save us from difficulty regarding the identity of this particular pure object; except to say that if this is all that makes it acceptable for Descartes to resort to the notion of pure objecthood, it would seem to follow that God is unique in the further respect that only he can be a pure object; which (though no doubt it is not conclusive) undermines the analogy with triangles and the like to which Descartes appeals.

A word or two first about this analogy and the use to which it is put by Descartes. On the face of it there is no obvious reason why Descartes should restrict pure objecthood (or givenness) to entitles capable of furnishing us with necessary truths, any more than there was any very obvious reason why Plato should not have had a form of Hair or Dirt. Kenny extracts two arguments on this point. One is against giving Meinongian status to self-contradictory entities like the round square; the other is against extending the scope of the Ontological Argument to include such objects as the existing golden mountain. Kenny holds that Descartes has a 'more intelligible' case if Meinongian being is denied to fictional as well as to self-contradictory objects; I am not sure, but I think he would also say that Descartes would or should have denied it also to non-fictional contingent entities like tables and chairs. It is ascribable therefore only to beings with 'true and immutable essences, i.e. those about which non-trivial truths can be proved a priori'.

Let us take the case to which Descartes confines himself, viz. that of geometrical objects. The triangle with its nature is *given*; what is meant by this? Part at least of what is meant is that the geometer is not someone who *invents* but someone who *discovers*. And what he discovers is independent of the actual existence of triangular objects in the world; we know that the interior angles of a triangle add up to 180 degrees before we consider whether there are any genuinely triangular objects. It is obviously not possible, I would suggest, to point with the same confidence to any theological proposition that is similarly demonstrable before we know whether God really exists or not. I am not arguing that Descartes' interpretation of the status of geometrical truths is correct; but if it is at all plausible it is because we feel confident that there are mathematical truths that are independent of the real existence of triangular things; and their very independence is the source of the 'givenness' of their subjects. It is not correspondingly obvious what could be meant by saying that we know God is all-powerful but not whether any God really exists. Thus far, at least, the analogy breaks down; to assume the possibility of a body of theologically demonstrable truths is to assume God's real being in a way in which the belief in geometrical truths is not to assume the real being of triangles.

There is, however, one place where Descartes could more plausibly suggest that the analogy holds. Geometrical truths are *non-trivial* truths. We have to *discover* that the interior angles of a triangle add up to 180 degrees. Although this is contained within the triangle's essence, it is not so *obviously* contained within it that we do not have to investigate the triangle to discover it. In thinking of the triangle, we think of facts which entail that it has angles equal to 180 degrees, but do not think of this fact itself. This no doubt is a reason for speaking of mathematical objects as 'given'—whatever this means—rather than invented, since it seems odd to say that we can invent more than we know we are inventing. Similarly the argument is supposed to lead us to the recognition that God's essence involves existence, even though this fact is not immediately obvious and requires some reflection on the essence of God (as the all-perfect being) to be made clear. So although the case for regarding God as having the 'given' status necessary to be the bearer of an essence to investigate seems quite hollow when compared with the case for saying this of the triangle, if the case is granted the analogy between uncovering God's real existence from within that essence and uncovering the non-defining properties of the triangle might seem plausible enough. For God's real being turns out to be one of the perfections by which that essence is in general terms first defined.

So far, of course, we have not touched upon the standard objection to this argument, viz. that existence, not being a predicate, cannot be classed among God's perfections. Here Kenny is surely misleading. The argument that existence is not a predicate he construes as follows: 'The objection "existence is not a predicate" amounts to this: "exists" cannot be a predicate because if it is false of any subject then there is no such subject for it to be false of.' Now if this were what the objection amounted to, a resort to provisional Meinongian status for God while we mustered our predicates would avoid it. But the objection amounts rather to the claim that existence cannot be included in the essence or nature *ascribed to* any entity, *whatever* metaphysical status that entity has to have to carry its essence. But only if existence can be so included can God's existence be a necessary truth, and only if it can be so included can arguments I and II be valid.

(It might be thought that this is only true in the case of argument I, and not true in the case of II. But only if existence is a perfection can there be any reason to say that God would want to have it; so II depends on the same assumption).

II

Recent discussions of the Ontological Argument have served to make it clear that the Kantian adage that existence is not a real predicate is at best a clumsy summation of partial insights. The peculiarities of the concept of existence have been further explored by many, but there has always seemed to be a point at which the supposed refutation of the Ontological Argument rested on an arbitrary (or, as Professor Malcolm has put it, 'intuitive') assertion that an existential statement cannot be a necessary truth, or that the existence of God cannot be included among his perfections. I do not claim to provide any demonstration where others have failed, but I do think that Mr. Kenny's examination of the way Descartes presents the argument can help us to see somewhat more clearly than before why it is a failure.

It seems possible to hold that there can be necessary existential propositions of which 'God exists' is an example, without holding that existence is a predicate, or that ascribing existence to something is informing us of its nature. An example of someone who would distinguish these is Professor Malcolm.[1] He argues that existence is not a property of God, but that necessary existence is. Necessary existence is a property ascribable to God in virtue of the fact that the assertion that God exists is a necessary truth. But if this latter is held along with the view that in saying God

[1] Norman Malcolm, 'Anselm's Ontological Arguments', *The Philosophical Review*, 69 no. 1 (January 1960), pp. 41–62.

exists we are not ascribing a predicate to him, I would think we would need to distinguish between holding that there can be at least one necessary existential assertion and holding that existence is a predicate.[2]

Descartes clearly seems to hold both that God's existence is a necessary truth, as Mr. Kenny argues, and that existence is part of the essence of God. While he needs both to maintain the analogy with mathematical truths, I think it is important to see that there is this prima facie difference between these two contentions. Professor Malcolm, very plausibly, has suggested it is absurd for critics of the Argument to concede that God's existence may be necessary and yet he still not exist. While this does *look* absurd, Shaffer has shown[3] that it can be construed in a way that is quite unexceptionable. In doing so he has shown grounds for thinking that (a) there can be necessary existentials, (b) 'God exists' might be one of them, (c) God might still not exist. I shall try to summarise his argument, using my own examples. 'Fictitious objects do not exist' or 'extinct creatures no longer exist' are necessary truths. One can build real existence into the subject of similar sentences, in the way *non*-existence is built into the subject of these. Such a move, however, does not prove the real existence of anything. Suppose there is someone who believes there are real unicorns as well as heraldic and mythical ones. Or suppose someone holds that Mr. Pickwick, in Dickens' novel, has a real-life counterpart, as Mr. Micawber has been said to have had. We could then frame the following two sentences: 'Real unicorns exist' and 'The actual Mr. Pickwick existed'. These could be interpreted as tautologies. Yet we would not feel persuaded that we had proved the existence of unicorns or of a historical counterpart to Mr. Pickwick. It is easy to see why: the sentences, though interpretable as tautologies, are ambiguous, and only in their non-tautologous sense do they inform us, or purport to inform us, about whether the world contains unicorns or ever contained an

[2] The distinction enables Malcolm to claim that Anselm's second argument is valid even though the first is not. The second, it will be remembered, is that God is proved to exist from the fact that he is the greatest being conceivable and that a being possessing necessary existence—i.e. a being who cannot not-exist—is a greater than one who lacks it, i.e. who can not-exist. One can only accept this argument and yet deny that existence is a predicate by holding, as Malcolm does, that the assertion that God exists has necessary status yet mentions none of God's properties.

[3] Jerome Shaffer, 'Existence, Predication, and the Ontological Argument', *Mind* 71 (1962), pp. 307–325.

actual Pickwick. *Qua* tautologies, they can merely serve to remind us that the concept of a real unicorn is the concept of a unicorn-that-actually-exists, and that the concept of the actual Mr. Pickwick is the concept of an allegedly historical figure. To tell us that reality, as opposed to fictional, status, is built into a concept is not to tell us that the concept has application. For this we need to be told that there *are* real unicorns, and that there *was* an actual Pickwick; and although our sentences above can yield this interpretation, when so interpreted they are not only not necessary truths, they are contingent falsehoods.

This certainly shows that the mere admission that there can be necessary existentials does not of itself prove the existence of any particular being. On the other hand, it still seems dogmatic to generalise from these examples to the conclusion that there can be no occasion when we are justified in the move from the conceptual to the real realm (or, presumably, from the Meinongian to the real realm) when we have a necessary existential assertion. A defender of the Ontological Argument would certainly react with some impatience to the above examples. But in order to proceed beyond the mere assertion that 'God exists' is different, one has to see *how* it is different.

One obvious difference is that the necessity of 'Real unicorns exist' is apparent at a glance, and that of 'God exists' (if this is indeed necessary) is not. The person who frames a sentence like 'Real unicorns exist' is self-consciously building the reality of the subject into the subject-term; yet the man who says that God exists may be quite unaware that the proposition he expresses is a necessary one. But this obvious difference does not explain anything, and is by itself usable by either side. For if there is ever any point in uttering necessary existentials like 'Real unicorns exist' it is presumably because some people can forget that real existence is built into the concept of real unicorns and need to have it recalled to them. And the fact that it may take a longer or shorter time to make clear what is included in a particular concept does not seem to have any conclusive bearing on the question of whether the person who uses it put it there gratuitously in the first place. So it becomes more clear that Descartes, if Mr. Kenny interprets him correctly here, showed great tactical perception in wanting to class 'God exists' not with *all* necessary truths, but with those like 'The triangle has interior angles equal to 180 degrees'. He would no doubt dismiss 'Real unicorns exist' as on a par with 'The existent golden mountain exists'. Suppose we ask what it is that the proposition about the triangle has to recommend it that the one about the existent golden mountain does not have. The answer would be that we feel uncomfortable about saying that the triangle's having angles equal to 180 degrees is put into the concept of the triangle before we start; we want to say (at least according to Descartes, and it is surely plausible) that we *discover* it to be a part of the nature of the triangle, even though it follows deductively from earlier propositions in which *we* seem to define what that nature is. In order to avoid the embarrassments attendant upon classing 'God exists' along with 'The existent golden mountain exists' or 'Real unicorns exist', therefore, it is necessary to add something to the claim that it is a necessary existential. It has to be a necessary existential of a special sort: one whose necessity derives from a purported examination of the nature of the being, God, to whom real existence is being ascribed. The Ontological proof does not merely need to say that it is logically necessary that God is. It is, after all, logically necessary that all real beings are. It has to say that it is necessary that God is because he is the sort of being that he is, viz. the sort of being who—*is*.

To maintain this, one would have to hold that existence is, or can be, a predicate in the way Kant said it could not be. The Proof needs both that there can be necessary existentials and that at least one of these can be construed as reporting the nature of God. Though Malcolm is right to distinguish them, he is mistaken in thinking that one can use the Ontological argument without holding both of them.

So far I have been distinguishing between the view that there can be necessary existentials and the view that existence is a predicate. It might be suggested that an additional distinction is needed—one between the view that existence is a predicate and the view that existence can be part of the nature of something. Surely these are not the same: are there not occasions when a predicate, P, might apply to a subject, S, without our wanting to say that P names part of the nature of S? I think that insofar as we can make any clear distinction here, it would be irrelevant in discussing the Ontological Proof. For I think we would have to base our distinction upon the difference between essential and accidental predicates. One can hold that a predicate, P, applies to a subject, S, and yet does not name part of the nature of S, if 'nature' means something close to 'essence'—in other words, if S could still be the sort of being it is even if P did not apply to it. (Sometimes, of course, the word 'nature' is used in a less stringent way, so that one could hold that P named part of the nature of S without believing that S would cease to be S if P were withdrawn; but in this case I can discern no difference between saying that P names part of the nature of S and just saying that P is a predicate applying to S.) In discussing the Proof I propose to ignore this distinction. For one thing, it is usually held in discussions of divine attributes that the distinction between essential and accidental characteristics vanishes in God's case. For another, it is clear that if existence is said to be a predicate that can apply to God, it has to be construed further as an essential one for 'God exists' to emerge as a necessary truth.

III

I want now to ask what can be made of the claim that it is God's nature to be (that real being is part of God's essence) so that *God* could not not-be. What sort of discovery is this claim alleged to report?

(1) The statement that P is part of the essence of S may merely mean that nothing could be called S unless it was agreed to have P. And whatever else it means, it would seem to *entail* this. So—no man could be called a bachelor unless he were unmarried; no being could be called God unless he were omnipotent; no being could be called God unless he existed.

At once we are in difficulties. As these stand, they are one and all false. Married men have been referred to, and some have even referred to themselves, as bachelors. Beings that were not omnipotent have been referred to as God. To deal with facts like these, we have to say that no one who was speaking sincerely and using words correctly, would refer to anyone as a bachelor unless he were an unmarried man; and no one who was speaking sincerely and using the word 'God' as a 17th century Christian used it would call a being 'God' unless that being were omnipotent.

This, of course, is inadequate also. We could quite easily call a married man a bachelor with complete sincerity and without misusing words, if we had made a mistake. And we could quite easily, with sincerity and without the misuse of words, call a being God who was not omnipotent—if we thought that being *was* omnipotent.

Let us now look at: no being could be called God unless it existed. This could be read as a special application of a general principle that nothing can be accorded any title unless it exists. This principle is refuted by the sincere and correct application of a predicate to any being mistakenly thought to exist by the speaker. If, of course, a philosopher were to hold that the sort of case mentioned did not refute the principle, this thesis would either prevent correct application of innumerable titles besides 'God' or prove the real existence of innumerable title-holders besides God.

The same would seem to follow from another possible reading of the claim that nothing could be called God unless it existed: that to accord the title to a non-existent being would be to involve oneself in self-contradiction. This claim certainly marks out 'God' for special status, but would also apply to our uninteresting actual Mr. Pickwick. If I were to call someone 'the actual Mr. Pickwick' and thus use that phrase not to talk about the concept of the actual Mr. Pickwick but as the correct title of someone, then I could be argued to be involved in self-contradiction if I then went on to say that the actual Mr. Pickwick did not exist.

Here it might be argued that this blatant form of self-contradiction would not in fact be uttered; that anyone who believed that there was no actual Mr. Pickwick would use the sentence 'The actual Pickwick does not exist' to speak only of the concept of that person, and that anyone who believed there was such a person would not use the sentence. Yet there is, the argument might run, a very common use of 'God does not exist' which is, in spite of appearances, self-contradictory; and it is *this* that is special about the concept of God, and *this* which could be used to unpack the claim that it is God's nature to be. Unfortunately, however, the claim that God's non-existence is a concealed contradiction is not clearly different from the claim that his existence is a necessary truth; and we have already seen that in order to establish this the Ontological Argument needs to appeal to the nature of God as One Who Is; an appeal we are now finding ourselves trying to articulate by reference to the very conclusion it has to be used to establish.

It would seem that we are not able to *explain* the thesis that it is God's nature to exist by reference to the view that only an existing being can correctly be called 'God'. For either this view is false or it fails to distinguish the divine case sufficiently from many others.

(2) Perhaps saying that it is God's nature to be is to be understood as saying that God does not just have existence, but has *necessary* existence. What, however, does *this* mean? For the purposes of the Proof it is clear that whatever it means to say that it is God's nature to be, it has to mean something that implies that if we understood the nature of God we would see that it not only was not the case that he did not exist, but could not be. But saying God has necessary existence does not supply us with this requirement. (a) It may mean merely that 'God exists' is a necessary truth. But we have already seen that if this is all that it means it fails to distinguish this necessary existential from others that clearly do not prove the real being of anything. So this reading is at least insufficient for the purpose. (b) So, saying God has necessary existence rather than *mere* existence means more than that 'God exists' is necessary. But the more which it means cannot be that God's existence is uncaused, or that God is incorruptible. For although, doubtless, it is necessarily true that God is uncreated and incorruptible, this does not show (as indeed Mr. Kenny argues) that it is not the case that he could not-exist. It merely shows that if he does exist he could not be caused to cease to and was not caused to. The notions of uncausedness and logically necessary being are quite independent—after all, it may be a necessary truth that the real Mr. Pickwick exists, but that does not make him uncaused or incorruptible. Only the fictional Mr. Pickwick is immortal. So it still seems that in the context of the proof the admission of necessary existentials needs to be supplemented by the appeal to the claim that God's nature involves existence, and does nothing to explain it.

(3) But if 'It is God's nature to be' does not just mean 'Nothing can be called God which does not exist', nor ' "God exists" is a necessary truth', nor 'God's existence is uncaused', what does it mean? For if it only means one or other of these things the proof collapses. Surely, the reply may go, it merely means that God's existence is *demonstrable*, in that it can be shown to follow from some other assertion about God's nature which is itself a necessary truth. But from what necessary truth about God is his real existence alleged to follow? According to Descartes it follows

from the truth that God possesses all possible perfections. This only follows if existence is one such perfection. I am unable, however, to see what can be meant by saying that P is a perfection in a subject S and yet is not part of the nature of S—unless 'S is P' is allowed to be merely contingently true. But this seems to mean that the demonstration that God exists presupposes the acceptance, and therefore the understanding, of the claim that it could be the nature of an entity to be. So this in turn cannot be explained in terms of the demonstrability of the being of God, since this demonstration rests on an appeal to it.

IV

I have tried to argue that at least Descartes' version of the Ontological Argument rests upon an appeal to the proposition that existence is of the essence of God. On the assumption that this claim needs some explanation, I have looked at some possible readings of it. I suggest that if any of the readings I have examined is correct, the proof collapses, either because God's real existence does not follow from the premises thus understood, or because the argument becomes circular. I can hardly think that the alternatives I have explored are exhaustive ones; and it is clear that I have produced no demonstration that they are. We are still, at best, in the realm of incomplete and partial insights. But we can at least wonder about the clarity of the move Descartes makes when he derives God's real existence from the fact that real existence cannot be separated from his nature. And if this wonder is not just perverse, it would seem to follow that the real difficulty of the Ontological Argument is not met by supplying God with Meinongian being so that he can then have a nature: the difficulty lies in including existence in that nature.

I have said nothing about the doctrine of Meinongian being itself, and I am happy to leave the general discussion of such doctrines to others. I would only say again that although it is possible to see Descartes' reasons for appealing to it, and for restricting it to entities whose natures are reported in necessary truths, this merely means that we can see how his appealing to it and restricting it in this way helps out his argument. It does not mean that one can detect any good grounds for adopting a doctrine of Meinongian being, or for restricting its application when one has adopted it. The true and the useful have a habit of being different. Of course, special grounds might be invented for accepting Meinongian being in God's case. Perhaps it too is a mode of existence that no self-respecting perfect being could possibly be without. But the only wise reaction to this potential move is 'Sufficient unto the day. . . .'

COMMENT

BERNARD WILLIAMS

Mr. Kenny deals favourably for a lot of his paper with Meinongian 'pure objects', and dismisses them in the end principally, if not solely, for the reason that no principles of individuation can be provided for them.

I think, however, that earlier, and fatal, difficulties beset the account of such objects. A pure object is said to have just those properties which can be established by non-trivial argument *a priori*. This can be put by saying: a pure object of type F possesses just those properties which are possessed *necessarily* by any F.

I shall use the expression 'the Polygon' to mean a certain ideal object; the expression 'polygon' will mean what it usually means.

Under certain geometrical restrictions, no doubt, which need not concern us here, we can assert truly:

(1) Necessarily, any polygon has either an even or an odd number of sides.

By the principle for determining the properties of ideal objects, it follows that

(2) The Polygon has either an even or an odd number of sides.

Consider now these propositions

(3) The Polygon has an even number of sides;

(4) The Polygon has an odd number of sides.

Evidently, neither of (3) and (4) is true. For, by the principles, the only way in which the Polygon can be F is by its being the case that any polygon is necessarily F ; and it is false that any polygon necessarily has an even number of sides, and false that any polygon necessarily has an odd number of sides.

Can we go directly from saying that (3) and (4) are not true, to saying that they are false? Perhaps not—it is less than totally clear what the rules here are. If we can, then we have a straight contradiction about the Polygon. Even if we cannot, we have a break-down in inference; for one would suppose that from (2) it followed that one or the other of (3) and (4) must be *true*.

A further consequence follows from this state of affairs. From the fact that neither (3) nor (4) is true, together with (1), there follows (5) No polygon is the Polygon, or (6) The Polygon is not a polygon.

Results of this kind are likely to be obtainable with any 'pure object'. They seem to provide a conclusive objection to the idea that by having the additional property of existence a 'pure object' could *turn into* an object of the type in question.

The general shape of those results might also suggest what is wrong with the whole enterprise: that it is utterly misguided to try to represent as singular and categorical and about peculiar objects, propositions which are indeed what they seemed to be when we started: general and hypothetical, and not about peculiar objects.

Comment

ERNEST SOSA

The distinction between true and immutable natures on the one hand, and fictional ones on the other, is essential to the Cartesian ontological argument. Were it not for that distinction, any such argument would be reduced to absurdity by Russell's ontological proof of an existent golden mountain. (An existent golden mountain that does not exist is inconceivable. Hence, . . .) Descartes' only defense appears to be that God has a true and immutable essence whereas an existent golden mountain does not. What then is it to have a true and immutable essence? Kenny's first suggestion (on page 24) is grounded on the assumption that for Descartes a triangle inscribed in a square does have a true and immutable essence. But this supposed ground is only shifting sand. In one and the same passage, in his 'Reply to Caterus',

Descartes both accepts and rejects the truth and immutability of the nature of a triangle inscribed in a square. Indeed, in a passage from the 'Reply . . .' quoted by Kenny (on page 33), it is stated categorically that a triangle inscribed in a square has '. . . no true and immutable essence.'

Nor is Kenny's other suggestion entirely convincing. He explains as follows '. . . the difference between true and immutable essences on the one hand, and fictitious essences on the other. If F is part of the true and immutable essence of G it is impossible for us to conceive of a G which is not F. If, on the other hand, we can conceive of a G which is not F, then even though we can make up the notion of a G which is F, this will be a fictional essence and not an immutable essence. . . . An existent golden mountain, then, does not have a true and immutable essence, and therefore no conclusion can be drawn about its existence. God, unlike the existent golden mountain, is no fiction, because we can prove *a priori* that what has the properties of God has also existence though we cannot prove *a priori* that what has the properties of a golden mountain has also existence.' (See page 33). The ending of this passage appears to miss the point of the beginning. Although '. . . we cannot prove *a priori* that what has the properties of a golden mountain has also existence', we *can* prove *a priori* that what has the properties of an *existent* golden mountain has also existence. And, moreover, we cannot conceive of an existent golden mountain that is not existent. What distinguishes God from an existent golden mountain is hence not this, but rather that the (simple) properties of God hang together in a way in which the (simple) properties of an existent mountain do not. This comes out in a suggestion of Kenny's at the beginning of the passage. 'If . . . we can conceive of a G which is not F, then even though we can make up the notion of a G which is F, this will be a fictional essence and not an immutable essence.' The suggestion here is that an essence is true and immutable only if each of its (simple) components, except possibly one, follows from the conjunction of the others. This does appear to be Descartes' own view:
. . . when I think of a winged horse, or of a lion actually existing, . . . I easily understand that I can on the contrary think of a horse without wings, of a lion as not existing . . . , and so forth, and that hence these things have no true and immutable nature. ('Reply to Caterus.')

Finally, I draw a conclusion from Kenny's last suggestion that yields further points in its favor. If an essence is true and immutable only if each of its (simple) components, except possibly one, follows from the conjunction of the others, then each true and immutable nature can be reduced to at least one of its (simple) components (by dropping, step by step, each of the others). Therefore, if God has a true and immutable essence, some one of his essential (simple) properties should entail each of the others. And indeed Descartes goes so far as to choose a (simple) property which on his view exhausts the nature of God, to wit, *omnipotence*. This he does in the conclusion of his 'Reply to Caterus', where he writes as follows:

> Because we cannot think of God's existence as being possible, without at the same time, *and by taking heed of his immeasurable power*, acknowledging that he can exist by His own might, we hence conclude that he really exists and has existed from all eternity; for the light of nature makes it most plain that what can exist by its own power always exists. And thus we shall understand that necessary existence is comprised in the idea of a being *of the highest power*, not by any intellectual fiction, but because it belongs to the true and immutable nature of that being to exist. We shall at the same time easily perceive that *that all-powerful being must comprise in himself all the other perfections that are contained in the idea of God, and hence these by their own nature and without any mental fiction are conjoined together and exist in God.*

(The italics are mine. I have relied so heavily on the 'Reply to Caterus' because the objection made by Caterus is essentially the same as the one made by Russell.)

Reply

ANTHONY KENNY

In response to Professor Penelhum I should perhaps insist that I do not think Descartes' argument is valid. It fails, I contend, principally because Meinongian objects are indefensible. I agree with Penelhum that if we give Descartes enough rope he will hang himself; I was arguing merely that he should be given more rope than he is usally given.

Unlike Penelhum, I think that non-trivial *a priori* truths about God can be proved whether or not God exists. One such is mentioned by Malcolm: God cannot begin to exist. Anyone who finds insoluble the problem of evil must think that there are such truths: e.g. that no benevolent and omnipotent God could make a world such as the one we live in. It seems to me that these truths are not mere truths about language any more than Pythagoras' theorem is.

I agree with Penelhum that 'the geometer is not someone who invents but someone who discovers' is a less misleading way of saying part of what is meant by 'the triangle with its nature is *given*'. Existence theorems in mathematics prove, I think, what Descartes would call *givenness* rather than what he would call *existence*. In private conversation with Professor Körner after the meeting I came to see that the identity of essence and existence which, for Descartes, was peculiar to God is in fact a feature of all mathematical entities as nowadays naturally conceived. This was not so for Descartes because of the concrete way in which he understood mathematical existence: for a triangle to exist is for there to be a triangular body; for a number n to exist is for there to be n concrete objects.

I do not follow Penelhum's argument that even if existence is a predicate it cannot be an essential one. I agree that existence could not be the *only* essential property of an object; existence, considered as a property, is as it were too thin to build up a nature. But if we accept that there are Meinongian objects, which can have, among their properties, that of existence, I do not see why there cannot be a Meinongian object to whom existence is essential. For Descartes the essence of an object is constituted by properties which it cannot cease to have: and any being which could cease to exist would not be God. I agree with Penelhum— and so, I have tried to show, would Descartes—that 'the notions of uncausedness and logically necessary being are quite independent'; but this tells not against Descartes' argument but against Malcolm's.

Professor Malcolm misunderstands my paper in seven ways.

(1) He says 'Kenny concludes that a triangle might be given even if no one ever thought of a triangle'. I did not conclude this: I claimed that Descartes assumed it.

(2) He says 'my first (small) comment is that Kenny has not

made me understand what it is for something to be *given* without being *thought of*. The main point of half my paper was that one must take this distinction seriously if one was to make sense of Descartes' argument. The main point of the other half of the paper was to say that the ultimate incomprehensibility of the distinction makes Descartes' argument fail. Much of Malcolm's first section is taken up with showing that what I said was (allegedly) true of given objects is false of objects of thought. I agree.

(3) Malcolm says that Descartes distinguishes between ideas as objects of thought and ideas as acts of thought. This is correct but irrelevant; for the idea of a chimaera is an object of thought no less than the idea of a triangle; but the triangle is given while the chimaera is not.

(4) Malcolm suspects 'that Kenny has made the error of assuming that if one is thinking of a triangle, one must be thinking of a triangle *that exists*'. On the contrary, I take it as an obvious truth that one can think of what does not exist. One can also prove theorems about what does not exist. Meinong's assumption of pure objects was a faulty theory to explain the former truth; Descartes' assumption of 'given' objects was a misguided move to account for the latter truth.

(5) I do not see that Malcolm anywhere takes account of the remark I quoted from Descartes that my thought imposes no necessity on things. What, on Descartes' view, imposes necessity on my thought of a triangle when no triangle exists? To this question, I reply: the given triangle. Malcolm makes no reply.

(6) Malcolm says 'if Descartes meant the subject of the sentence "God exists" to be something that is "beyond being", then he could not use the sentence to assert that God exists'. I do not think he can have noticed the passage I quoted from Meinong, that to say an object is beyond being and not being 'is not to say that an object can neither be nor not be'.

(7) Malcolm says he sees no merit in my 'claim that it is impossible to provide criteria of identity for objects of thought'. I made no such claim; I was talking about given objects, not objects of thought; and the passage I quoted from Quine concerned unactualised possibles. Malcolm's own criterion of identity for objects of thought seems much too strict: Malcolm and I are both thinking of the same thing if we are both thinking, say, of

Bismarck; and this may be so without either of us 'stipulating' any properties for Bismarck.

The connection which Malcolm points out in his second section between the ontological argument and the doctrine of simple natures is, I think, very interesting and important. But I would like to see it made clear what is the relation between the simple *natures* of the *Rules* and the simple *notions* of the letters to Elizabeth. Are these entities identical? If so, are they mental or extra-mental? If not, are the former extra-mental and the latter their mental counterparts? One would need to know the answer to these questions in order to assess the relevance of the doctrine to the interpretation of the Ontological argument.

It seems to me that the argument defended by Malcolm in his third section could be used to prove the necessary existence of all sorts of entities, e.g. of a 100-year-old baby. It is inconceivable that a 100-year-old baby should begin to exist; for if it began to exist, it would not be a hundred years old. Whatever can be conceived to exist but does not exist, can be conceived as beginning to exist, according to Anselm. Consequently, a hundred-year-old baby cannot be conceived to exist and yet not exist. If, therefore, a hundred-year-old baby can be conceived to exist, he exists of necessity. But there is nothing inconceivable in the notion of a hundred-year-old baby (why shouldn't a race take a very, very, long time to reach maturity?) Hence, a hundred-year-old baby exists necessarily. In this argument, one may substitute for 'hundred-year-old baby' any description such as 'Lucretian atom' or 'Aristotelean planet' and thus prove the necessary existence of anything which is by definition sempiternal.

Both Professor Sosa's points seem to be well taken. He is correct in pointing out that Descartes seems to have been unable to make up his mind whether a triangle inscribed in a square has a true and immutable essence. Perhaps this hesitation may be taken to indicate a dim perception of the problems of Meinongian status.

Sosa is also right that my formulation of the difference between true essences and fictitious essences is faulty. It might be amended to read as follows. 'Let E be an essence which can be defined by the predicates F and G, so that something possesses the essence E if it is both F and G. If F is part of the true and immutable essence E it is impossible for us to conceive of a G which is not F.

If, on the other hand, we can conceive of a G which is not F, then even though we can make up the notion of a G which is F, this will be a fictional essence and not an immutable essence.'

This will, I think, accurately reflect Descartes' view in the reply to Caterus. None the less, it will not save Descartes from Sosa's criticism, for a reason which was pointed out to me by my wife. On this criterion, a square will not have a true and immutable essence, as is clear if we let E be the essence of a square, and for F put 'equilateral' and for G 'rectangle'. This difficulty cannot be answered by distinguishing, as Sosa suggests, between simple and complex properties, unless we take the implausible view that *being triangular* is simple and *being rectangular* is complex.

I agree with Professor Williams' exposition of the problems engendered by the Pure Polygon, and am grateful to him for bringing out that Meinongian objects are even more intractable than I had realised.

Symposium II

ON EVENTS AND EVENT-DESCRIPTIONS

R. M. MARTIN

In his *Aspects of Scientific Explanation*[1] Hempel distinguishes in a rough way between what he calls 'sentential' and 'concrete' events. A scientific explanation is regarded as 'a potential answer to a question of the form "why is it the case that p?", where the place of "p" is occupied by an empirical sentence detailing the facts to be explained.' Such 'facts' or events—Hempel does not distinguish them—are, e.g., 'that the length of a given copper rod r increased during the time interval 9.00 to 9.01 a.m. or that a particular drawing d from a given urn produced a white ball'. Such events, being described or describable by phrases containing sentences, are called 'sentential'.

A 'concrete' event, on the other hand, is not described or specified by a sentence but rather by 'a noun phrase such as an individual name or a definite description as, for example, "the first solar eclipse of the twentieth century", "the eruption of Mt. Vesuvius in A.D. 79", "the assassination of Leon Trotsky", "the stock market crash of 1929".' Noun-phrases of this kind let us call hereafter *event-descriptions*.

By an 'individual name' Hempel presumably means a name of an individual, and by a 'definite description', presumably a Russellian description of the usual kind, namely, an expression of the form 'the one x such that $(-x-)$', where 'x' is an individual variable and '$(-x-)$' is a sentential function containing 'x' as its only free variable. Individual names are presumably either proper names or abbreviations for descriptions. (If they are some other sort of expression, we do not know what.) In either case, they name *individuals*, whatever the individuals of our discourse are. Let us assume, for present purposes at least, that they are either concrete, spatio-temporal chunks of matter (in accord with Carnap's *reism*) or physical objects in some sense (in accord with

[1] The Free Press, New York and Collier-Macmillan Limited, London, (1965), pp. 421 f.

physicalism).[2] This seems the most natural assumption to make in the philosophy of science, and one surely with which Hempel would not cavil.

We might instead take our individuals as just events *sui generis* in some sense, but just what such events are, as contrasted with concrete or physical objects, is not too clear. In any case, we should note that the 'definite descriptions' and 'individual names' Hempel mentions do not strictly stand for individuals in the sense of concrete or physical objects but rather for events in some sense. A solar eclipse, whatever it is, is not a concrete or physical object, nor is the eruption of Mt. Vesuvius nor the market crash of 1929. Nor for that matter is the increase in length of a copper rod nor a drawing d of a ball from an urn. These are all events, in some vague sense at least.

The usual language-systems, employing a first-order logic with perhaps identity, seem well-suited to handle concrete or physical objects. How now can events be handled within them? How is time-flow to be handled, for talk of time is surely endemic to event-talk? And over and above events, we surely wish to admit physical or concrete objects anyhow. And if so, precisely how are such objects related to events? It is, after all, the concrete or physical objects to which the events happen, as it were. Solar eclipses take place in time as between certain macroscopic objects; the eruption of Mt. Vesuvius is an event involving a certain geographic entity; an assassination is of a certain physical individual; and so on.

Perhaps the language in which we talk of solar eclipses, for example, can be constructed in such a way as *not* to contain names or variables for the macroscopic objects, sun, moon, earth, etc., involved. It is not clear precisely what would be gained in trying to avoid such reference, however, i.e., in allowing our variables and names to refer only to events. The more natural course, as has been suggested, seems to be to admit concrete or physical objects as the fundamental ones and then try to build up events in some fashion as constructs. This seems never to have been done explicitly. The result is that phrases such as the event-descriptions Hempel mentions seem never to have been analyzed *au fond* and given an exact logic. An attempt to analyze them within the framework of a reistic or physicalistic language is made in this paper.

[2] See especially *The Philosophy of Rudolf Carnap* in *The Library of Living Philosophers*, La Salle, Ill.: Open Court Pub. Co. (1963), pp. 869 ff.

But first we should ask whether Hempel's distinction between two kinds of events, 'sentential' and 'concrete', can be maintained. Whatever *facts* are,[3] they are not to be confused with events, as Ramsey was perhaps the first to point out. 'The event which . . . is called "the death of Caesar" [quotes added] . . . should no more be confused with the fact that Caesar died,' he writes, 'than the King of Italy [in 1927] should be confused with the fact that [in 1927] Italy has a King.'[4] 'The death of Caesar' is presumably an event-description just as 'the King of Italy in 1927' is an individual description. They are intimately related respectively with the 'facts' given by the statements 'Caesar died' and 'Italy had a King in 1927'. Just as the King was a human person, not a fact, so is Caesar's death an event and not a fact. Hempel's 'sentential' events thus seem best regarded as facts, and we are left with only his 'concrete' events to worry about. Facts and events we shall wish to keep quite separate.

The very label 'sentential' suggests reference to language whereas 'concrete' suggests reference to objects. The two labels are thus not on a par, as it were. Strictly then, it seems, we have only one kind of event but two ways of speaking of them. Further, it seems easy to pass from one way of speaking to another. For example, 'that the length of a given copper rod r increases during the time interval 9.00 to 9.01 a.m.' easily becomes the event-description 'the increase of the length of the copper rod r during the interval 9.00 to 9.01 a.m.,' and conversely. 'That Trotsky was assassinated' becomes 'the assassination of Trotsky' and conversely. It is thus not clear why Hempel thinks that we have two kinds of events rather than merely two ways of talking about them.

Let us go on to try to construct a 'model' for events within the familiar reistic or physicalistic object-language.

The first item to note is that events involve time. As event is a happening *at a time*. The assassination of Trotsky took place at a time, etc., etc. Thus some underlying theory of time-flow seems needed in order to handle events.[5] Let 't', 't_1', etc., be variables ranging over the time-stretches admitted in such a theory.

[3] See the author's 'Facts, What They Are and What They Are Not', *American Philosophical Quarterly*, 4 (1967), pp. 269–280.
[4] F. P. Ramsey, *The Foundations of Mathematics*, New York: Harcourt, Brace and Co. (1931), pp. 138 ff.
[5] Cf. the author's *Intension and Decision*, Englewood Cliffs, N. J.: Prentice-Hall (1963), pp. 41 ff.

That events involve time fundamentally has been well recognized. Broad, for example, brought this out clearly when he noted that an event is 'anything that endures at all, no matter how long it lasts or whether it be qualitatively alike or qualitatively different at adjacent stages of its history'. This he finds contrary to common usage 'but common usage has nothing to recommend it in this matter.... We usually call a flash of lightning or a motor accident an event, and refuse to apply this name to the history of the cliffs of Dover. Now the only relevant difference between the flash and the cliffs is that the former lasts for a short time and the latter for a long time. And the only relevant difference between the accident and the cliffs is that, if successive slices, each of one second long, be cut in the histories of both, the contents of a pair of adjacent slices may be very different in the first case and will be very similar in the second case. Such merely quantitative [qualitative?] differences as these give no good ground for calling one bit of history an event and refusing to call another bit of history by the same name.'[6]

In accord with the familiar trichotomy of individuals (or objects), classes or virtual classes[7] (or properties taken extensively), and relations or virtual relations (also taken extensively), we may distinguish three kinds of events, *object-events*, *property-events*, and *relation-events*. This seems a reasonable trichotomy, and using it will help clarify the whole subject of event-talk. These we may regard as the most fundamental kinds of events. Other derivative kinds can then be built up in terms of them.

Object-events are in effect enduring objects with the time of endurance made explicit. Thus the cliffs-of-Dover-at-time-t constitute an object-event, as do the-cliffs-at-time-t_1, where t_1 is any continuous (non-scattered) part of t. The physical cliffs are the 'content' of the events, and t or t_1 are their respective times. An object-event is completely described in terms of its 'content' (or object) and time. The longest object-event whose content consists of the cliffs of Dover is the-cliffs-of-Dover-at-t, where t is their whole temporal life-span.

The notion of an ordered pair has been extolled by Quine, in

---

[6] C. D. Broad, *Scientific Thought*, London: Routledge and Kegan Paul (1923), p. 54.
[7] See the author's 'The Philosophic Import of Virtual Classes', *The Journal of Philosophy* 61 (1964), pp. 377–387.

Word and Object, as a kind of philosophic paradigm.[8] Suppose we have two entities at hand and wish to regard them as in some sense one, and wish also to distinguish the order in which they are taken. It is convenient and natural then to form the ordered pair of the two given objects and to regard the ordered pair as the one object we desire. Quine speaks only of *real* ordered pairs in the sense that they are values for variables. 'A notion of ordered pair would fail of all purpose', he writes, 'without ordered pairs as values for the variables of quantification'. But this seems not the case. *Virtual* ordered pairs are also useful, as well as virtual ordered triples, etc. In fact, events may be regarded here as virtual ordered n-tuples of a certain kind. More particularly, object-events are to be regarded as virtual ordered pairs, the first member of the pair being the 'content', the second the time.

Let 'x', 'y', etc., be the individual variables. Let

'$\langle x, t \rangle$' be defined as 'the virtual relation between y and t_1 where $y=x$ and $t_1=t$' (or, symbolically '$yt_1{}^{\jmath}$ $(y=x \cdot t_1=t)$').

The enduring object or object-event x-throughout-t might then be regarded merely as $\langle x, t \rangle$. But this would not quite do. For suppose t were a time outside the life-span of x. What kind of an 'event' would this be? What sort of an event would

$$\langle \text{Leon Trotsky, A.D. 79} \rangle$$

be? Possibly a *null* event? Well it seems better to rule out such pairs by requiring that t be a *part* of x in the special sense in which times may be said to be parts of physical objects.[9] Let 't P x' express that the time t is a part in this sense of the physical object x. Then we may write

'$\langle x, t \rangle^e$' for '$yt_1{}^{\jmath}(y=x \cdot t_1=t \cdot t_1 \text{ P } y)$'.

Such pairs are called virtual *event*-pairs, and hence the superscript 'e'. The *definiendum* here gives us a general notation for event-descriptions of object-events.

Let us turn now to the sort of events described by noun clauses such as 'the eruption of Mt. Vesuvius in A.D. 79', 'the assassination

---

[8] The Technology Press of the Massachusetts Institute of Technology and New York and London: John Wiley and Sons (1960), pp. 270 ff.
[9] See the author's 'Of Time and the Null Individual', *The Journal of Philosophy* 62 (1965), pp. 723–736. Note incidentally that for the handling of just object-events, we do not strictly need *ordered* pairs. We could make virtual cardinal couples do equally well.

of Leon Trotsky', 'the death of Caesar', and so on, *property-events*, as we shall call them. Each of these seems to involve not only a physical object and a time, but also a property, or more particularly, a property as relativized to a time (whether the time is explicitly mentioned or not). The clause 'the eruption of Mt. Vesuvius in A.D. 79' involves not only Mt. Vesuvius, the time A.D. 79, but the property of erupting. (Of course erupting here could be regarded as a relation between Mt. Vesuvius and a time, but we shall speak of it as a property instead.) 'The death of Caesar' involves Caesar, the property of dying, and a time. Property-events are not to be regarded merely as virtual ordered pairs, but rather as virtual ordered triples, one member of which is a property. But even this will not quite do, for 'the death of Caesar at t'—we bring in the time for explicitness—does not describe an event unless Caesar actually died at t once and once only. Likewise 'the eruption of Mt. Vesuvius in A.D. 79' is not an event-description unless Mt. Vesuvius actually erupted in A.D. 79 once and once only. So some provision must be made, in our handling of this second kind of events, to assure that the events described actually take place uniquely at the proper times. Let

'$\langle x, F, t \rangle^e$' abbreviate 'the virtual triadic relation among y, G, and t_1 such that $y=x$, $G=F$, $t_1=t$, and y has G at t_1' (or, symbolically, '$yFt_1 \ni (y=x \cdot G=F \cdot t_1=t \cdot Gyt_1)$').[10]

All such triples, virtual ordered event-triples of a special kind, constitute the domain of property-events. The triple $\langle$Caesar, dies, $t\rangle^e$ is the event *the death of Caesar* provided Caesar actually died uniquely at t. The definiendum here gives us a general notation for event-descriptions of property-events provided 'Gyt_1' is properly construed.

Of course we might wish to subdivide property-events into various kinds, depending upon whether the relevant property is a quality, such as *red*, *green*, *warm*, etc., an action-property such as *walks*, *dies*, *accelerates*, etc., or some other kind of property. Action-properties seem to give rise to events in a very natural way, qualities in a less natural way. Examples of action-properties we have already met with in the examples considered. But how about

[10] 'F' and 'G' are not to be regarded as property variables, but rather as standing for virtual classes. And ordered triples, one component of which is a virtual class, are to be formed *mutatis mutandis* precisely as ordered triples all of whose components are invididuals. Cf. 'The Philosophic Import', p. 380.

'this leaf's being green at t'? Should this be regarded as a property-event-description? Surely no harm arises from so regarding it. But even so, restrictions could be imposed upon the set of properties allowed to give rise to property-events, if desired.

The 'content' of a property-event now consists not only of an individual, but of a property as well. Properties are taken here extensively, it will be recalled, so that neither intensionalism nor Platonism in any form need be involved in our reference to them. Properties are to be regarded as completely determined when the objects having them are determined. Equivalently, properties here may be regarded as virtual classes.

In a similar way dyadic relations give rise to relation-events. The event-description 'the revolution of the earth around the sun at t', for example, clearly involves the relation of revolving with the two arguments the earth and the sun.[11] Here virtual ordered quadruples of a certain kind are needed. The 'content' of a dyadic relation-event must of course include the relevant relation as well as the relevant objects which stand in that relation.

In a similar way we pass on to event-descriptions involving triadic relations, and so on. 'John's giving a ring to Mary,' for example, involves the triadic relation of giving. 'X's selling y to z in recompense for w dollars' involves a quadratic relation. And so on.

Greater sophistication in the handling of time would no doubt be required if we were to consider more closely the actual language of physics. It is not clear that this would require any fundamental change, however. The simple topology of time used here seems common to all theories of time, absolute, relative, epochal, or whatever, in the sense that it can be built up within them. If a

---

[11] We should be careful not to confuse relational events with the relations involved in those events. Russell apparently confuses these in 'On Denoting' (*Logic and Knowledge* London George Allen and Unwin (1956), pp. 53–54), where he regards 'the revolution of the earth around the sun' as the description of an 'entity'. 'If "aRb" stands for "a has the relation R to b",' he writes, 'then when aRb is true, there is such an entity as the relation R between a and b: when aRb is false there is no such entity. . . E.g., it is true (at least we will suppose so) that the earth revolves around the sun and false that the sun revolves around the earth; hence "the revolution of the earth around the sun" denotes an entity, while "the revolution of the sun around the earth" does not denote an entity'. Russell does not apparently distinguish here, as he should have, between the *relation* of revolving and the *event* consisting of the earth's revolving around the sun at some time. Instead of speaking here of the relation R between a and b as an entity, Russell should have spoken of the ordered quadruple among R, a, b, and a time, these ordered quadruples themselves being a kind of quadratic relation.

metric for time is introduced, this would merely complicate the treatment rather than alter it fundamentally. Also, the class of object-languages here is so wide that the presumption seems justified that any domain of knowledge however complex can be accommodated within them. And although we have stuck to rough, more or less common examples, as is customary, this does not render the mode of treatment necessarily inadequate as applied to more sophisticated material.

We need not claim that the kinds of events discriminated, object-, property-, and relation-events, are the only basic kinds, but this does seem likely. Each of these kinds can be subdivided in various ways as desired. Also events in any one kind can be combined to form longer or more complex ones in appropriate ways.

Let us consider the motor accident, of which Broad speaks. This may perhaps be analyzed as a succession of property-events involving the same object but with differing properties. Without over-simplifying too much, let us assume the motor accident involves just the four successive times, $t_1, \ldots, t_4$. At t_1 the motor car is running along smoothly. At t_2 it skids, at t_3, it hits the embankment, at t_4 it overturns. Here we have a succession of property-events, with the respective properties of running along smoothly, skidding, hitting the embankment, and overturning. (We recall that an individual x stands in the logical product ($R \frown S$) of two virtual dyadic relations R and S to y if and only if x bears R to y and also x bears S to y.[12] And similarly for triadic virtual relations. And similarly for virtual relations in which one of the relata is itself a virtual class.) The accident then may be regarded as the logical product of the four property-events mentioned. Let us call such a product the *successive product* of the property-events concerned. Let D, S, H, and O be the respective properties here and let m be the motor vehicle. Then the respective property-events are $\langle m,D,t_1 \rangle^e$, $\langle m,S,t_2 \rangle^e$, $\langle m,H,t_3 \rangle^e$, and $\langle m,O,t_4 \rangle^e$. Their successive product, the motor accident under review, is then

$$(\langle m,D,t_1 \rangle^e \frown \langle m,S,t_2 \rangle^e \frown \langle m,H,t_3 \rangle^e \frown \langle m,O,t_4 \rangle^e).$$

We have enormous freedom, of course, in building up successive products of property-events. Presumably any successive

[12] Cf. *Principia Mathematica*, *23.02.

product with the same object is a property-event. The most interesting cases are those in which there is significant or unusual change in the properties involved. These constitute the 'events' of common speech. Similar remarks apply to relation-events. Object-events, on the other hand, are presumably not recognized as 'events' in our common language.

Hempel remarks, in a footnote, that he is not certain as to how a necessary and sufficient condition for the *identity* of 'concrete' events is to be formulated. If events are assimilated to 'facts', there is a real problem here for the latter are in some sense intensional entities. The condition under which two 'facts' are to be regarded as identical is controversial.[13] We have been urging, however, that events are not to be regarded as intensional entities. Hence a clear-cut notion of identity between events ought to be forthcoming. And it is, in the virtual treatment, namely, merely as identity between the virtual entities involved. We must not confuse the event with the event-description. We may vary the description without therewith varying the event. One and the same event may have alternative event-descriptions, just as one and the same individual may have alternative Russellian descriptions. In the case of object-events, there seems no problem. $\langle x,t \rangle^e$ is identical with $\langle y,t_1 \rangle^e$ just in case $x=y$ and $t=t_1$.

When we turn to property- or relation-events, we might be puzzled as to the condition of identity. It is not clear, however, that such puzzlement would be fruitful. Puzzles ought not to be multiplied beyond necessity. If F and G are one and the same property or virtual class, surely $\langle x,F,t \rangle^e$ and $\langle x,G,t \rangle^e$ are one and the same property-event. To be sure, we *describe* it differently. But here likewise, we must not confuse the event, the actual going-on in nature, with the terms we use to describe it.

The phrase 'occurrence of an event' is frequently used by philosophers of science without analysis and in ways which are logically jarring. In discussions of causal explanation, for example, it is frequently alleged that 'there are general laws ... in virtue of which the occurrence of the causal antecedent ... is a sufficient condition for the occurrence of the explanandum event'. It might be argued that we all know well enough what this says and hence there is no need for analysis of the key phrases. But the step from

---

[13] Cf. I. Scheffler, *The Anatomy of Inquiry*, New York: Alfred A. Knopf (1963), pp. 57 ff., and the author's 'Facts'.

using 'occurrence of an event' to 'existence of a thing' is a short one, and it may be that similar confusions attach to each. No sophisticated philosopher would use 'existence of a thing' without qualms, or at least without recognizing that at best the phrase is to be traced back to quantifiers in some suitable fashion. The same, we wish to urge, is true of 'occurrence of an event'. Of course events occur, there is nothing else for them to do. The phrase is thus at best periphrastic. To say of an event that it occurs is merely to say that it contains a time factor, and this is always true. To say that an event occurs is like saying that an object exists, bad philosophical grammar no doubt being involved in both cases.

In the foregoing treatment, an event-description is taken in such a way as always to describe an event. A kind of 'existence' condition, as it were, is built into the *definientia*. In the case of object-events the existence condition is that the time involved be a part of the object constituting the 'content'. In the case of property-events, the existence condition is that the object involved have the relevant property at the time. And similarly for relation-events. Also a kind of unicity condition, that there is *at most one* event being described, is implicit in the uniqueness of the respective objects, properties, relations, and times. This treatment of event-descriptions thus differs in this respect from that of Russellian descriptions, in which either the existence or unicity condition may fail. It is interesting to note that, if it is thought fit, we may drop the existence conditions here and incorporate them rather into the *definientia* of general predicates for 'is an object-event', 'is a property-event', and so on. Conceivably there might be some advantages to such a treatment. We need not therewith recognize a realm of non-events in some fashion. Rather we would have a means of singling out expressions for those ordered pairs, triples, etc., which do describe events from those which do not.

Let

'ObjEv R' abbreviate '(Ex) (Et) ($R=\langle x, t\rangle$. x P t)'.

To say that a dyadic virtual relation R *is an object-event* is then to say that there is an x and a t such that R is the virtual ordered pair $\langle x, t\rangle$ and x P t. Similarly

'PrpEv Q_F' abbreviates '(Ex) (Et) ($Q=\langle x, F, t\rangle$. Fxt)'.

A triadic virtual relation Q (involving the property F in a certain way) *is an event determined by the property F* provided there is an x and a t such that Q is the virtual triple $\langle x,F,t \rangle$ where Fxt. (Note that because we cannot quantify over properties or virtual classes, the 'F' must occur in the *definiendum* as a parameter.) And similarly for relation-events.

It remains to consider the restrictions upon quantifiers over events. Concerning object-events there is no problem. Quantification over them is achieved by quantifying the respective variables for individuals and times. In the case of property- and relation-events, the expressions for virtual classes and virtual relations cannot be quantified. Nonetheless, schemata may be given, with the individual and time-variables directly quantified, which give substantially the effect of quantifiers. Thus some general principle concerning property-events, for example, could be written as a schema thus:

$$(x)(t)(\text{PrpEv}\langle x,F,t\rangle \supset -\langle x,F,t\rangle -),$$

for all 'F'. The effect of having universal quantifiers over property-events is achieved to some extent in this way. Of course the use of schemata does not give the full effect of quantifiers but at least suffices for many purposes.

We note that events are sharply to be distinguished from facts, not because of the virtuality involved but because events are not spoken of *nominally*. Facts are to be regarded as nominal entities having an intensional structure, and hence can be referred to only indirectly.[14] Events, on the other hand, we can refer to directly. We cannot say that events are real things in the world, although their 'contents' are. But this circumstance is surely sufficient to give them enough reality and concreteness. Further, we note that talk of events can take place within the physicalistic or reistic object-language, provided it contains a theory of temporal flow. Fact-talk is through and through meta-linguistic, taking place only within a suitable semantical meta-language. Events are temporally dated, facts are not. Events are clear-cut extensional entities, facts are intensional constructs. Both, however, are fictitious in the sense of being handled only virtually.

A final comment. We have urged throughout the *virtual* treatment of ordered n-tuples. But nothing of a technical nature hinges fundamentally upon this. We may, if we wish, regard

[14] See again 'Facts'.

events rather as the corresponding *real* ordered n-tuples, presupposing now some kind of set- or type-theory as the basic logic. In so doing, we would gain the full effect of quantifiers over each kind of events. We would thus gain a 'model' for events within the richer resources of a reistic or physicalistic object-language built upon a set- or type-theory. Such richer languages being widely preferred to the narrower ones utilizing only the virtual theory of classes, it is interesting to note that the suggestions here may also be of interest for Platonistic reism and physicalism.

DONALD DAVIDSON

I

There is a more or less innocent sense in which we say that a sentence refers to, describes, or is about, some entity when the sentence contains a singular term that refers to that entity. Speaking in this vein, we declare that 'The cat has mange' refers to the cat, 'Caesar's death was brought on by a cold' describes Caesar and his death, and 'Jack fell down and broke his crown' is about Jack and Jack's crown. Observing how the reference of a complex singular term like 'Caesar's death' or 'Jack's crown' depends systematically on the reference of the contained singular term ('Caesar' or 'Jack') it is tempting to go on to ask what a sentence *as a whole* is about (or refers to, or describes), since it embraces singular terms like 'Caesar's death' in much the way 'Caesar's death' embraces 'Caesar'. There is now a danger of ambiguity in the phrases 'what a sentence refers to' or 'what a sentence is about'; let us resolve it by using only 'refers to' for the relation between patent singular terms and what they are about, and only 'corresponds to' for the relation between a sentence and what it is about.

Just as a complex singular term like 'Caesar's death' may fail of reference though contained singular terms do not, so a sentence may not correspond to anything, even though its contained singular terms refer; witness 'Caesar's death was brought on by a cold'. Clearly enough, it is just the true sentences that have a corresponding entity; 'The cat has mange' corresponds to the cat's having of mange, which alone can make it true; because there is no entity that is Caesar's death having been brought on by a cold, 'Caesar's death was brought on by a cold' is not true.[1]

These gerunds can get to be a bore, and we have a way around them in 'fact that' clauses. The entity to which 'The cat has mange' corresponds is the cat's having of mange; equivalently, it is the fact that the cat has mange. Quite generally we get a singular term for the entity to which a sentence corresponds by prefixing 'the fact that' to the sentence; assuming, of course, there are such entities.

Philosophical interest in facts springs mainly from their promise for explaining truth. It's clear that most sentences would not have the truth value they do if the world were not the way it is, but *what* in the world makes a sentence true? Not just the objects to which a sentence refers (in the sense explained above), but rather the doings and havings of relations and properties of those objects; in two words, the facts. It seems that a fact contains, in appropriate array, just the objects any sentence it verifies is about. No wonder we may not be satisfied with the colourless 'corresponds to' for the relation between a true sentence and its fact; there is something, we may feel, to be said for 'is true to', 'is faithful to', or even 'pictures'.

To specify a fact is, then, a way of explaining what makes a sentence true. On the other hand, simply to say that a sentence is true is to say there is some fact or other to which it corresponds. On this account, '*s* is true to (or corresponds to) the facts' means more literally '*s* corresponds to a fact'. Just as we can say there is a fact to which a sentence corresponds when the sentence is true, we can also say there is a true sentence corresponding to a particular fact; this latter comes down to saying of the fact that it is one. English sentences that perhaps express this idea are 'That the cat has mange is a fact' and 'It is a fact that London is in Canada', and even 'London is in Canada, and that's a fact'. It is evident that we must distinguish here between idioms of at least two sorts, those that attribute facthood to an entity (a fact), and those

---

[1] For simplicity's sake I speak as if truth were a property of sentences: more properly it is a relation between a sentence, a person and a time. (We could equally well think of truth as a property of utterances, of tokens, or of speech acts.) I assume in the present paper that when truth is attributed to a sentence, or reference to a singular term, the suppressed relativization to a speaker and a time could always be supplied; if so, the ellipsis is harmless.

that say of a sentence that it corresponds to a fact (or 'the facts'). Let us use the following sentences as our samples of the two sorts of idiom:

(1) That the cat has mange is a fact.
(2) The sentence 'The cat has mange' corresponds to a fact.

Professor Martin says his analysis is intended to apply to sentences of the form 'So-and-so is a fact' where I suppose 'so-and-so' is to be replaced, typically, by a that-clause, and he suggests we interpret such sentences as saying of a sentence that it is true (non-analytically—but I shall ignore this twist). Which of the two idioms represented by (1) and (2) is Martin analyzing? The sentences Martin says he wants to analyze apparently have the form of (1); his analysis, on the other hand, seems suited to sentences like (2).

Suppose we try the second tack. Then Martin's proposal comes to this: where we appear to say of a sentence that there is a fact to which it corresponds we might as well say simply that the sentence is true. There is nothing in this yet to offend the most devoted friend of facts. Martin has not explained away a singular term that ever purported to refer to a fact; on his analysis, as on the one the friend of facts would give, the only singular term in 'The sentence "The cat has mange" corresponds to the facts' refers to a sentence. Nor would the friend of facts want to deny the equivalence of '*s* is true' and '*s* corresponds to a fact' when '*s*' is replaced by the name or description of a sentence. The friend of facts would, however, balk at the claim that this shows how, *in general*, to eliminate quantification over facts, or singular terms that refer to them. He would contend that it is only sentence (1) with its apparent singular term 'that the cat has mange' which clearly calls for an ontology of facts. Martin may reply that it is sentence (1) he had his eye on from the start. This reply leaves (2) out in the cold unless, of course, (1) and (2) can be given the same analysis. The partisan of facts will resist this idea, and plausibly, I think, on the ground that (2) is merely an existential generalization of the more interesting:

(3) The sentence 'The cat has mange' corresponds to the fact that the cat has mange.

Here Martin's attempt to treat facts as sentences cannot be made to work without reducing (3) to the statement that the sentence 'The cat has mange' corresponds to itself, and this cannot be right since (3), like (2), is clearly *semantical* in character; it relates a sentence to the world. Martin recognizes the semantic thrust in talk of facts, but does not notice that it cannot be reconciled with his analysis of (1).

Martin's thesis that we do not need an ontology of facts could still be saved by an argument to show that there is at most one fact, for the interest in taking sentences like (3) as containing singular terms referring to facts depends on the assumption that there is an indefinitely large number of different facts to be referred to: if there were only one, we could submerge reference to it into what might as well be considered a one-place predicate.[2] And an argument is handy, thanks to Frege, showing that if sentences refer at all, all true sentences must refer to the same thing. Suppose the sentence 'London is in Canada' refers to some fact; we will not change the reference if we substitute a logically equivalent sentence, say 'The class of those such that they wear hats and London is in Canada is identical with the class of hatwearers'; nor will we change the reference if in this last sentence we replace the singular term 'the class of those such that they wear hats and London is in Canada' by another singular term with the same reference, say 'the class of those such that they wear hats and snow is white'; but our resulting sentence is 'The class of those such that they wear hats and snow is white is identical with the class of hatwearers', and it is logically equivalent to 'Snow is white'. Since 'Snow is white' was chosen as a random sentence with the same truth value as 'London is in Canada', we must conclude that the reference of every true sentence is the same; there is at most one fact.[3]

We may then with easy conscience side with Martin in viewing 'corresponds to a fact', when said a sentence, as conveying no more than 'is true'. What should we say of the sentences like (1) that appear to attribute facthood to entities? As we have seen, such sentences cannot be analyzed as being about sentences. Bearing in mind the unity of fact, we might say (1) affirms The

[2] For a more general treatment of 'ontological reduction' by incorporation of a finite number of singular terms into predicates, see Quine's contribution to the present volume and 'Ontological Reduction and the World of Numbers' in *The Ways of Paradox*, New York, 1966, p. 203.

[3] Assuming someone wears a hat, of course. For the argument and discussion, see A. Church, *Introduction to Mathematical Logic*, Vol. I, Princeton, 1956, pp. 24–25. This argument depends on taking classes and their names seriously, so Martin may not like it; though, if I am right, he needs it.

Great Fact, or tells The Truth, by way of one of its infinite tags, 'The cat has mange'. We could equally well accept the universe with 'That London is in Canada is a fact'. Equivalently, we could have simply said 'The cat has mange' or 'London is in Canada'. So, on my account, 'The sentence "The cat has mange" corresponds to the facts' comes out 'The sentence "The cat has mange" is true', but 'That the cat has mange is a fact' comes out just 'The cat has mange'; not at all the same thing.[4]

Sentence (3) seemed at first more interesting than (2), but only because it was thought that there were facts to which a true sentence does not correspond. Frege's argument shows otherwise by proving there is one fact at most; thus (3) is equivalent in import to (2). We already recognized that (2) would be less misleading if taken as simply attributing truth to the sentence 'The cat has mange'; the same insight may now be appropriately extended to cover (3).

It will be seen that I am in full agreement with Martin's main conclusion about facts: we don't want them in order to give a coherent account of the English idioms we have been discussing. My main quarrel with Martin is that he has conflated two problems, with the consequence not only that he has neglected one of the problems, but also that he mistakenly thinks sentences may be viewed as ersatz facts.[5] This last source of disagreement might, I think, breed further dispute if we were to go on to discuss sentences about propositional attitudes. As long as we think there are a multitude of facts for sentences to correspond to, it is natural to suppose facts among the objects of propositional attitudes: facts can be learned, forgotten, challenged, resented, accepted, explained, and so on. But the line I have followed to show we don't need facts to analyse sentences like (1), (2), and (3) depends on showing that there is one fact at most, so there can be no application of this solution to the problem of analyzing sentences about propositional attitudes. For the propositional attitudes require a multitude of objects if they require any: there would have to be as many facts as there are true propositions. Martin apparently hopes we can

[4] I think that failure to observe the distinction between these two cases is the cause of some of the endless debate whether attributions of truth are redundant.

[5] I confess I do not understand how the apparatus of virtual classes and relations helps Martin's analysis. He needs genuine singular terms referring to expressions, and once the subject is an expression and not its reference I don't see how it matters, for present concerns, whether the expression has one or another of various logically equivalent forms.

take sentences about propositional attitudes as being about sentences. I confess I am sceptical, but since he does not pursue the subject here, neither shall I.

Facts, for Martin, are so intensional they may be treated as sentences; for me they are so extensional they melt into one. The result, as it happens, is the same: as a rich domain of entities corresponding to, but different from, sentences, facts don't exist. In the case of events, I start out in general accord with Martin, for I agree that event-talk is thoroughly extensional.[6] But on the central issue, whether events exist, we are quite at odds, for unlike Martin, I do not see how to interpret some of our plainest language without supposing there are events.

It is often assumed or argued (though not by Martin) that events are a species of fact. Austin, for example, says, 'Phenomena, events, situations, states of affairs are commonly supposed to be genuinely-in-the-world. . . . Yet surely of all these we can say that they *are facts*. The collapse of the Germans is an event and is a fact—was an event and was a fact'.[7] Reichenbach even treats the words 'event' and 'fact' as synonyms, or so he says.[8] The pressure to treat events as facts is easy, in a way, to understand: both offer themselves as what sentences—some sentences at least—refer to or are about. Causal laws, we are told, say that every event of a certain sort is followed by an event of another sort. According to Hempel, the sentence 'The length of copper rod r increased between 9.00 and 9.01 a.m.' describes a particular event.[9] In philosophical discussion of action these days we very often learn such things as that 'Jones raised his arm' and 'Jones signalled' may describe the same action, or that an agent may perform an action intentionally under one description and not under another. It is obvious that most of the sentences usually said to be about events contain no singular terms that even appear to refer to events, nor are they normally shown to have variables that take events as values when put over into ordinary quantificational notation. The

---

[6] By this I mean only that most sentences about events do not show referential opacity. But descriptions of anything, and hence of events, may make use of opaque constructions. This happens when we describe mental events (that is, describe events as mental): remembering, perceiving, acting with an intention, deciding, coming to believe, learning. The need for this important caveat was brought to my attention by Ronald Butler.
[7] John Austin, 'Unfair to Facts', in *Philosophical Papers*, Oxford, 1961, p. 104.
[8] Hans Reichenbach, *Elements of Symbolic Logic*, New York, 1947, p. 269.
[9] Carl Hempel, *Aspects of Scientific Explanation*, New York, 1965, p. 421.

natural conclusion is that sentences as wholes are supposed to describe or refer to events, just as they were said to correspond as wholes to facts.

Reichenbach has worked at this idea in some detail, and a glance at his theory will be instructive. Suppose Jones was born on the 4th of July: we may symbolize this as usual:

(4) Born (Jones, 4th of July)

or, equivalently according to Reichenbach:

(5) $(\exists x)(x$ is the fact that Born (Jones, 4th of July))

where the variable ranges over events and 'is the fact that' is an operator which, when adjoined to a sentence, forms a predicate of events. Knowing that the 4th of July is Independence Day we readily infer 'Born (Jones, Independence Day)', from (4), and so ought to be able to infer '$(\exists x)(x$ is the fact that Born (Jones, Independence Day))', from (5). The principle involved, that we may substitute co-extensional singular terms in sentences following 'is the fact that' is just what is needed to set Frege's argument in motion again to prove that if 's' and 'r' are sentences alike in truth value, then:

(x) (x is the fact that $s \leftrightarrow x$ is the fact that r).

That is, all events are identical (there are no 'false events'). This result was to be expected; it is the fate of attempts to extend a normal theory of reference to sentences.

Martin does not fall into this common trap, for although he constructs singular terms for events from the material of a sentence, he does not have the sentence itself refer to an event. His procedure is to view an event as an ordered n-tuple made up of the extensions of the n-1 singular terms and the n-1-place predicate of a true sentence. So 'Leopold met Stephen on Bloomsday' gives us the singular term '$\langle M, l, s, b\rangle$' which refers to Leopold's meeting of Stephen on Bloomsday provided Leopold did meet Stephen on Bloomsday. I shall ignore the further step which eliminates ordered n-tuples in favour of virtual ordered n-tuples; the difficulties about to appear are independent of that idea.[10]

Given the premise that Bloomsday is June 16, 1904, we may infer from 'Leopold met Stephen on Bloomsday' the sentence 'Leopold met Stephen on June 16, 1904', and, events being the

[10] Substanially the same analysis of events as Martin's has recently been given by Jaegwon Kim, 'On the Psycho-physical Identity Theory', *American Philosophical Quarterly*, 3 no. 3 (1966), pp. 227–235. Kim does not take the extra step from real to virtual ordered n-tuples.

ordered *n*-tuples they are, Leopold's meeting of Stephen on Bloomsday is identical with Leopold's meeting of Stephen on June 16, 1904. This is surely as it should be so far; but not, I'm afraid, farther. Not every encounter is a meeting; according to the story, some encounters between Leopold and Stephen are meetings and some are not. But then by Martin's account no meeting is identical with an encounter, though between the same individuals and at the same time. The reason is that if any encounter is not a meeting, $\langle E, l, s, b \rangle$ is not identical with $\langle M, l, s, b \rangle$. Indeed, Leopold's first meeting with Stephen on Bloomsday in Dublin cannot be identical with Leopold's first meeting with Stephen on Bloomsday (since a four-place predicate can't have the same extension as a three-place predicate); nor can a meeting between Stephen and Bloom be identical with a meeting between Bloom and Stephen (since entities will be ordered in a different way). No stabbing can be a killing and no killing can be a murder, no arm-raising a signalling, and no birthday party a celebration. I protest.

Martin's conditions on identity of events are clearly not necessary, but are they perhaps sufficient? Again I think the answer is no. Martin correctly remarks that on his analysis the expressions that are supposed to refer to events refer to one entity at most; but are these entities the events they should be? Suppose Leopold met Stephen more than once on Bloomsday; what unique meeting does Martin's ordered *n*-tuple pick out? 'Leopold's meeting with Stephen on Bloomsday', like Martin's '$\langle M, l, s, b \rangle$', is a true singular term. But there is this difference, that the first refers to a meeting if it refers to anything, while the second does not. Being more specific about time will not really mend matters: John's kissing of a girl at precisely noon is not a unique kissing if he kissed two girls simultaneously. Martin's method cannot be systematically applied to form singular terms guaranteed to pick out a particular kissing, marriage, or meeting if anything; but this is easy, with gerund phrases, in English.

Martin's mistake is natural, and it is connected with a basic confusion about the relation a sentence like 'Leopold met Stephen on Bloomsday' or 'Casesar died' and particular events like Leopold's meeting with Stephen on Bloomsday or Caesar's death. The mistake may be encapsulated in the idea (common to Martin and many others) that 'Leopold met Stephen on Bloomsday' comes to the same as 'Leopold's meeting with Stephen on Bloomsday occurred' or that 'Caesar died' may be rendered 'Caesar's death took place.' 'Caesar's death', like 'Leopold's meeting with Stephen', is a true singular term, and so 'Caesar's death took place' and 'Leopold's meeting with Stephen occurred' are true only if there was just one such meeting or death. But 'Caesar died' is true even if Caesar died a thousand deaths, and Leopold and Stephen may meet as often as they please on Bloomsday without falsifying 'Leopold met Stephen on Bloomsday'.

A sentence such as 'Vesuvius erupted in 79 A.D.' no more refers to an individual event than 'There's a fly in here' refers to an individual fly. Of course there may be just one eruption that verifies the first sentence and just one fly that verifies the second; but that is beside the point. The point is that neither sentence can properly be interpreted as referring or describing, or being about, a particular eruption or fly. No singular term for such is in the offing. 'There's a fly in here' is existential and general with respect to flies in here; 'Vesuvius erupted in 79 A.D.' is existential and general with respect to eruptions of Vesuvius in 79 A.D.—if there are such things as eruptions, of course.

Here I am going along with Ramsey who, in the passage quoted by Martin, wrote ' "That Caesar died" is really an existential proposition, asserting the existence of an event of a certain sort, thus resembling "Italy has a King", which asserts the existence of a man of a certain sort. The event which is of that sort is called the death of Caesar, and should no more be confused with the fact that Caesar died than the King of Italy should be confused with the fact that Italy has a King.'[11] This seems to me nearly exactly right: facts, if such there are, correspond to whole sentences, while events, if such there are, correspond to singular terms like 'Caesar's death', and are quantified over in sentences such as 'Caesar died'.[12]

Martin says he doubts that 'Caesar died' must, or perhaps even can, be construed as asserting the existence of an event of a certain

---

[11] Ramsey, *Foundations of Mathematics*, New York, 1931, pp. 138 ff.

[12] Austin blundered when he thought a phrase like 'the collapse of the Germans' could unambiguously refer to a fact and to an event. Zeno Vendler very shrewdly uncovers the error, remarking that 'in as much as the collapse of the Germans is a fact, it can be mentioned or denied, it can be unlikely or probable, it can shock or surprise us; in as much as it is an event, however, and not a fact, it can be observed and followed, it can be sudden, violent, or prolonged, it can occur, begin, last, and end.' This is from 'Comments' by Vendler on a paper by Jerrold Katz, both printed in *The Journal of Philosophy* 62 (1965), pp. 590–605.

sort. I want to demonstrate briefly first that it can, and then, even more briefly, why I think it must.

It can be done by providing event-verbs with one more place than we generally think necessary, a place for events. I propose that 'died' in 'Caesar died' be taken as a two-place predicate, one place for 'Caesar' and another for a variable ranging over events. The sentence as a whole then becomes '$(\exists x)$ (Died (Caesar, x))', that is, there exists a Caesar-dying event, or there exists an event that is a dying of Caesar. There is no problem in forming a singular term like 'Caesar's death' from these materials: it is '$(\imath x)$ (Died (Caesar, x))'. We may then say truly, though this is not equivalent to 'Caesar died', that Caesar died just once: '$(\exists y)$ ($y =$ $(\imath x)$ (Died (Caesar, x)))'; we may even say Caesar died Caesar's death: 'Died (Caesar, $(\imath x)$ (Died (Caesar, x)))'.

This gives us some idea what it would be like to treat events seriously as individuals, with variables ranging over them, and with corresponding singular terms. It is clear, I think, that none of the objections I have considered to Reichenbach's, Kim's, or Martin's analyses apply to the present suggestion. We *could* introduce an ontology of events in this way, but of course the question remains whether there is any good reason to do so. I have already mentioned some of the contexts, in the analysis of action, of explanation, and of causality in which we seem to need to talk of events; still, faced with a basic ontological decision, we might well try to explain the need as merely seeming. There remains however a clear problem that is solved by admitting events, and that has no other solution I know of.

The problem is simple, and ubiquitous. It can be illustrated by pointing out that 'Brutus stabbed Caesar in the back in the Forum with a knife' entails 'Brutus stabbed Caesar in the back in the Forum' and both these entail 'Brutus stabbed Caesar in the back' and all these entail 'Brutus stabbed Caesar'; and yet our common way of symbolizing these sentences reveals no logical connection. It may be thought the needed entailments could be supplied by interpreting 'Brutus stabbed Caesar' as elliptical for 'Brutus stabbed Caesar somewhere (in Caesar) somewhere (in the world) with something', but this is a general solution only if we know some fixed number of places for the predicate 'stabbed' large enough to accommodate all eventualities.[13] It's unlikely we shall

---

[13] Full credit should go to Anthony Kenny for emphasizing this problem in *Action, Emotion and the Will*.

succeed, for a phrase like 'by' can introduce an indefinitely large number of modifications, as in 'He hung the picture by putting a a nail in the wall, which in turn he did by hitting the nail with a hammer, which in turn he did by. . . .'[14] Intuitively, there is no end to what we can say about the causes and consequences of events; our theory of language has gone badly astray if we must treat each adverbial modification as introducing a new place into a predicate. The problem, you can easily persuade yourself, is not peculiar to verbs of action.

My proposed analysis of sentences with event-verbs yields an easy solution to this difficulty, for once we have events to talk about, we can say as much or as little as we please about them. Thus the troublesome sentence becomes (not in symbols, and not quite in English): 'There exists an event that is a stabbing of Caesar by Brutus event, it is an into the back of Casear event, it took place in the Forum, and Brutus did it with a knife'. The wanted entailments now go through as a matter of form.[15]

Before we enthusiastically embrace an ontology of events we will want to think long and hard about the criteria for individuating them. I am myself inclined to think we can do as well for events generally as we can for physical objects generally (which is not very well), and can do much better for sorts of events, like deaths and meetings, just as we can for sorts of physical objects, like tables and people. But all this must wait. Meanwhile the situation seems to me to be this: there is a lot of language we can make systematic sense of if we suppose events exist, and we know no promising alternative. The presumption lies with events.

R. J. BUTLER

Professor Martin's account of intensional logic reverses the usual process. Instead of regarding intensions as determining possibilities of class-membership, he maintains that intensions may be constructed in terms of a notion of analytic truth assumed within the object-language, and *ipso facto* that the theory of intensions is

[14] I am indebted to Daniel Bennett for the example.
[15] I have given a fuller exposition and defense of this analysis in 'The Logical Form of Action Sentences', forthcoming in *The Logic of Action and Preference*, edited by Nicholas Rescher, Pittsburgh, 1967.

a branch of the theory of extension. In an elegant proof Professor H. E. Hendry has shown that the system Martin advocated in *Intension and Decision* is open to the fatal objection that class constants designating the same class have the same intension.[1] In the paper under review[2] I have been able to find no indication that Hendry's objection has been met, despite the sustained appeal to nominal virtual classes; and of course this is crucial if we are to distinguish the fact that the author of *Waverley* lived at Abbotsford from the fact that the author of *Marmion* lived at Abbotsford. Although no general proof is forthcoming, it remains an open possibility that any attempt to construct intensions out of extensions will yield the result that class constants designating the same class have the same intension, and this of course would defeat the purpose of the enterprise. Certainly the onus is upon Professor Martin to show that Hendry's result can be avoided.

Professor Martin however is an ingenious man: we shall just have to wait and see if a piece which is to appear, called 'An Improvement in the Theory of Intensions', and another piece, which is an improvement of the 'Improvement',[3] turns the tables on his critics. Meanwhile I alight from his machine and climb back into my horse-drawn buggy,[4] in order to examine from that height cracks in his chassis. Professor Martin is not stipulating uses of 'fact' and 'event' for the purposes of his system, nor is he attempting to reconstruct a segment of fact-talk and event-talk. His is the more ambitious enterprise of telling us what facts as contrasted with events are and what they are not.[5] True, this is his aim, and he does not claim to have achieved this aim; but

[1] H. E. Hendry, 'Professor Martin's Intensions', *The Journal of Philosophy*, 62 (1965), pp. 432–4.
[2] That is, the paper submitted to the commentators before the meeting was held.
[3] These pieces have now appeared. The criticism stands.
[4] In the paper under review Martin had written: 'But one thing surely is clear at this late date: we cannot with impunity philosophize about facts in resolute laymanship and in disregard of the refined tools of modern semantics. To do so is to rely upon mere horse and buggy procedures, and to get only to the next town when we wish to go a great distance'. And again: 'No matter what facts are, they are surely not independent of truth, and the notion of truth seems most efficiently handled in terms of the modern semantic notion. Many analytic philosophers think they can avoid bringing in the semantic concept, and that some rather vague, pre-analytic notion will serve equally well. Well, perhaps so, back in the horse-and-buggy days. The view here is that the semantic notion cannot be avoided, and the sooner we get used to this the better for all of us.'
[5] The title of the paper under review was 'Facts, What They Are and What They Are Not'.

nevertheless his aim is to construct a system which, if it were successful, would pin down facts once and for all. Facts, we are told, 'are in some sense intensional entities', they 'are to be regarded as intensional entities having a nominal structure', and hence 'they can be referred to indirectly,' 'fact-talk being through-and-through meta-linguistic,' whereas 'events are clear-cut extensional entities,' they 'can be referred to directly,' event-talk 'can take place within the physicalist or reistic object-language, provided it contains a theory of temporal flow,' for 'events are temporally dated, facts are not.' Whatever the intrinsic merit of Professor Martin's system in its highly original attempt to derive virtually everything virtually, the fact remains that *at* this temporally dated stage in the evolution of our language the sharp contrasts he draws between facts and events fail to catch all-important nuances of talk about both. In the event *that* I can make good this claim, it will *become* clear *that* whatever is unfair to facts is also unfair to events.

Events are happenings, and there are intensional happenings as well as happenings which may be thought of either intensionally or extensionally. Concerning intensional happenings I would register a plea for mental events, and if in this I swim against the tide I had thought until I heard Professor Davidson's paper that I did so in the company of a stronger swimmer than I, for I fully agree with his contention in an earlier paper that 'states and dispositions are not mental events, but the onslaught of a state or a disposition is.'[6] There was a moment when I decided to accept the invitation to participate in this colloquium, and indeed when Professor Margolis put this to me he indicated that in the event *that* I decided to participate he would send me further information later. We discussed alternative symposia, and Margolis terminated the conversation with the words, 'In any event I shall ask you to do either the one or the other'. (The event in question concerned *the fact that* another philosopher, who unfortunately is not with us, might decide not to come.) 'In the event that you decide . . .', 'In any event if you decide . . .', 'In the event that you ask me . . .', 'In any event I shall ask you . . . ' are all so deeply imbedded in discourse that I find it difficult to understand why there should be such reluctance to accept moments of decision and moments of

---

[6] D. M. Davidson, 'Actions, Reasons and Causes', *The Journal of Philosophy*, 60 (1963), p. 694.

asking as intensional events: and there are many other mental events, or states now designated as 'propositional attitudes' which are demarcated by mental events, and which in turn can only be individuated and identified intensionally. My deciding at such-and-such a time to participate can be uniquely identified only in terms of what I decided then, that is in terms of the fact that I then decided that I would participate.[7] When one decides at a particular moment that one will do something, one is liable to be asked 'Was your decision a fact or an event?' and of course the answer depends upon whether one focusses on the moment of decision or what was decided. These we have just seen to be inseparable when one is uniquely identifying a moment of decision. It is therefore not surprising that the language enables us to play it either way, to treat the decision as either an event or a fact. Although in the present case there is a logical connection between the act of deciding and what was decided, in that one cannot uniquely identify the former without reference to the latter, this inability to give a clear-cut answer to the question 'Fact or event?' crops up in other contexts when one is not concerned with mental events and when this particular logical connection is not present.

Consider for example Ramsey's pronouncement:

The connection between the event which was the death of Caesar and the fact that Caesar died is, in my opinion, this: 'That Caesar died' is really an existential proposition, asserting the existence of an event of a certain sort, thus resembling 'Italy has a King', which asserts the existence of a man of a certain sort. The event which is of that sort is called the death of Caesar, and should be no more confused with the fact that Caesar died than the King of Italy should be confused with the fact that Italy has a King.[8]

Along with a host of other writers cited by Professor Martin, Ramsey believed that a fact is a true proposition, indeed, a true existential proposition. Note however the context in which this proposition appears. Ramsey had just remarked that a phrase like 'the death of Caesar' may be used in two quite different ways: 'ordinarily, we use it as the description of an event, and we could say that "the death of Caesar" and "the murder of Caesar" were two different descriptions of the same event. But we can also use

[7] Cp. Professor Davidson's fn. 6 above.
[8] F. P. Ramsey, *The Foundation of Mathematics*, London, 1931, p. 141.

"the death of Caesar" in contexts like "He was aware that Caesar had died",' where one might be aware of the fact that Caesar had died without being aware that he was murdered. So in point of fact, Ramsey saw that 'the death of Caesar' might serve either to describe an event or name a fact, but he thought that it would be obvious in any context which function the phrase was serving, and that its primary function is to describe an event. Had he taken an example like 'The assassination of Caesar precipitated significant constitutional changes within the Roman state' he would have seen that sometimes one just cannot say whether the phrase in question describes an event or names a fact, and that in such cases the question of primacy does not arise since the phrase, to purloin a metaphor from Professor Vendler, enters both batteries.

Consideration of cases like this led to Professor J. M. Shorter's diagnosis of the impasse between Austin and Strawson, a diagnosis which I regard as something of a breakthrough in that brand of philosophy caricatured here as resolute Oxford laymanship. Strawson, it will be remembered, aligned 'fact' with 'truth', whereas Austin aligned 'fact' with 'occurrence, state of affairs, etc., which is actual.' Shorter argues that exactly the same sort of doubt can be cast on the value of Austin's evidence as Austin casts on Strawson's. When Austin notes, for example, that we can say things like 'The collapse of France is a fact', he is suggesting the following line of thought: the phrase 'the collapse of France' refers to an event, we can say of this event that it is a fact, we can therefore say of an event that it is a fact, and this supports the view that 'is a fact' means 'is an occurrence, etc., that is actual'. To this Shorter tellingly replies: 'This argument depends upon the assumption that the phrase "The collapse of France" means the same in (a) "The collapse of France occurred in 1940" and (b) "The collapse of France is a fact". But in these two sentences the phrase 'the collapse of France' is not grammatically identical. For in (b) we can subsitute for it "that France collapsed", whereas in (a) we cannot do so. Again, we cannot infer from (a) and (b) 'A fact occurred in 1940". This is because the phrase "the collapse of France" does not mean the same in the two premisses.'[9] Shorter also draws attention to a feature characteristic of impasses between

[9] J. M. Shorter, 'Facts, Logical Atomism and Reducibility', *The Australasian Journal of Philosophy*, 40 (1962), pp. 286-7. Zeno Vendler later made the same point: cp. Davidson, *supra*, fn. 12.

rival paradigm case arguments, viz., the amount of common evidence which either side can draw upon. Does 'Verify your (alleged) facts' mean 'Check on the truth of the statements you allege to be true' or does 'verify' here mean 'check on the actuality of'? Again, in the case of 'an accomplished fact' 'accomplished' could mean 'made true by somebody's efforts'. Shorter's assessment of the impasse is not merely that given sufficient ingenuity it is generally possible to allege an ambiguity which one's opponent has overlooked, but also that both protagonists 'are almost invariably able to find further evidence in support of the allegation. In this way the occasional exceptions, where they cannot so defend themselves, appear to each as odd unimportant quirks of language which produce only very minor blemishes in the general pattern of usage.'[10]

In similar vein Professor Zeno Vendler's claim that causes correspond to results rather than events, 'cause' and 'result' both expressing the dependence of one fact upon another, is parried by Shorter with a sentence like 'The explosion was the cause of the accident'. In such a sentence, he says, 'there is, in the nature of the case, no answer to the question "Is the word 'explosion' being used in what Vendler calls an event-like sense or what he calls the fact-like sense?" ' And indeed in this particular sentence ' we cannot determine the sense (fact or event) of either "explosion" or "cause". For we can replace "the explosion" by a that-clause, or by "something which occurred earlier". We can replace "the cause of the accident" by either "loud" or "improbable".'[11] Vendler had emphasized, and the point is obviously important, that verb-nominalizations yield very different transformations. 'John's cooking is unlikely' yields 'It is unlikely that John cooks'. 'John's cooking is slow' yields 'John cooks slowly'. 'John's cooking is nutritious' yields 'What John cooks is nutritious.'[12] As Vendler puts it, a verb nominalization 'enters all the batteries. Only in a specific co-occurrence with certain sets of adjectives *or* with words like "effect", "result", "cause", and so on, does a nominalization become selective; only then does it belong to a battery.'[13] Shorter

[10] Ibid., pp. 290-1.
[11] J. M. Shorter, 'Causation, and a Method of Analysis', *Analytical Philosophy*, Second Series, ed. R. J. Butler, Oxford, 1965, pp. 156-7.
[12] Z. Vendler, 'Effects, Results and Consequences', *Analytical Philosophy*, First Series, ed. R. J. Butler, Oxford, 1962, pp. 4-5.
[13] Z. Vendler, 'Reactions and Retractions', ibid., p. 28.

points out that Vendler is mistaken in supposing that a nominalization becomes selective when it co-occurs with 'cause' for 'cause' itself enters more than one battery. And earlier in these remarks on Martin's bifurcation of facts and events I was suggesting that 'event' enters more than one battery. And Shorter has shown that 'fact' enters more than one battery.

Apparently in this argument the notion of 'battery' is eroding, but this is not really so. Vendler still has his three basic transformations, which one can label as one pleases. Let us call the 'fact-like' transformation 'A', the 'event-like' transformation 'B', and the 'object-like' transformation 'C'. Then it may be said that 'fact', 'event' and 'cause' enter both of the batteries A and B, not each with the same distribution, but each with sufficient entries into both to preclude membership of one only, and each with a significant number of indeterminate instances such that one just cannot say that one battery rather than another has been entered. The idea of a battery remains intact: from the fact that sometimes one cannot say that one battery rather than another has been entered it certainly does not follow that 'belonging to a battery' has entered more than one battery. True, it was a mistake to label batteries as 'event-like' and 'fact-like' since 'event' and 'fact' enter more than one battery; but batteries A and B remain distinct, the one yielding a noun clause which qualifies for a truth-value, the other yielding an adverbial clause which also qualifies for a truth-value. The contrast between the two batteries is *not*, as has been maintained in this symposium, that the one is propositional and the other is not.

What emerges, I think, is not a systematic ambiguity in 'event', 'fact' and 'cause', but rather a pattern of usage more complicated than we had imagined. The one thing we must not do in the light of this development is to foist upon a member of this family of inter-related concepts a preconceived theory, to wit, that a fact is to be regarded as a nominal entity having an intensional structure, which can be referred to only indirectly, fact-talk being through-and-through meta-linguistic; and then, having brought *this* theory to bear upon the facts, to distill by way of contrast the features of another member of the family, to wit, that an event is a clear-cut extensional entity, which can be referred to directly, that event-talk can take place within the physicalist or reistic object-language provided it contains a theory of temporal flow, events being temporally related whereas facts are not. If this line is pursued then sooner or later another Austin will come along and show how very fact-like events are; and as with the debate between Austin and Strawson, both protagonists will be wrong.

The matter, however, must not be allowed to rest here. One wants to know why such important words as 'fact', 'event' and 'cause' are able to enter different batteries. According to Shorter we should relinquish the quest for a core-meaning-cum-deviants when rival paradigms of usage present themselves, neither being conclusive, each claiming approximately the same amount of evidential support with an overlap of uses to which both parties lay claim. My own position is that if we had really arrived at the core meaning we would be able to illuminate the rival accounts and show why the impasse had occurred. It is not that Strawson might be right, or that Austin might be right, but that both have misidentified the type of meaning required. What is the peculiarity which has made the core meaning of 'fact' so elusive?

In his paper 'On Not Worshipping Facts' Mr. J. R. Lucas set out to attack the squirrel theory of history, 'the theory which holds that it is the duty of the historian to gather facts from county record libraries and deposit them again in university libraries.'[14] The burden of his attack is the absence of a unitary concept of fact. In science fiction, he points out, *the facts* which are organised into theories are facts on the one hand because they are not theories, and on the other hand are not facts because they are fiction; and legal facts likewise are facts because they are not moral pronouncements and are not facts because they are laws or the interpretations of laws. Although he believes that there is no unitary concept of fact, Lucas seeks 'some system in the ambiguity of word'. From the incontestable premiss that language is primarily a dialogue rather than a monologue, he rightly observes that in order for communication to proceed there must be points of agreement in the discussion. These points of agreement we call *the facts*. Any further point of agreement between protagonists become a fact in their subsequent discussions. 'That is to say,' writes Lucas, 'a fact is a fact relative to a given dispute, or relative to two or more persons at a given time arguing about a given point.'[15] Thus the

---

[14] J. R. Lucas, 'On Not Worshipping Facts', *The Philosophical Quarterly*, 8 (1958), pp. 153–4.
[15] Ibid., p. 146.

Theory of Evolution and the Theory of Special Relativity started by being speculations, then became hypotheses, developed into well-founded theories, and can now normally be described as facts. They are starting-points for further discussions: in the absence of counter-evidence there is no need to re-open the question of their truth. Lucas concludes his discussion by making facts relative to possible disputes in order to weaken their dependence on the particular issue in hand. 'A fact,' he says, 'is what a disputant would concede as true if he were a reasonable man living at that time.'[16]

Now I find this definition question-begging in the extreme. Quite apart from the appeal to sweet reason, as if 'reasonable men' were guarantors of truth, there is another respect in which as a definition it is faulty. Greater awareness is needed of the fact that a definiens must reproduce exactly that degree of abstraction or concreteness, of personality or impersonality, as is contained in the definiendum. As there are degrees of abstraction and degrees of impersonality, the demand for precision is likely to be exacting. When I say 'It is a fact that Stalin was assassinated in the Kremlin in 1953' there is no reference to the speaker or to any other disputant, actual or possible; nor does its being a fact depend upon what anybody, reasonable or unreasonable, would concede at this or any other time, nor is there any reference in stating it to be a fact to the grounds for believing it to be so. As a statement of fact it has a high degree of abstraction from disputants, actual and possible, and their grounds. This is one of the most singular things about fact-talk, that it proceeds at a fairly abstract and impersonal level. Lucas to some extent saw this when he said that since what we call *the facts* are points of agreement, there is no need in the absence of counter-evidence to re-open the question of their truth. And in making facts relative to possible disputes he was introducing precisely that modality which I think is contained in a claim that something is a fact, viz., that it is the kind of thing that can be established, or that can be explained. In accepting something as established or explained one also accepts the sufficiency of the conditions for establishing or explaining it, and what conditions count as sufficient changes from time to time. Therefore in saying that something is a fact one is claiming, without asserting, that there are *now* sufficient conditions for establishing it. Although

[16] Ibid., p. 160.

this is implicit in saying that something is a fact it is not part of the meaning of 'fact', for in saying that something is a fact we do not mention a time, nor do we mention the grounds themselves, nor do we mention that the grounds are sufficient, nor do we mention that it is *we* who consider the grounds to be sufficient. There are other ways, more personal and less abstract, of saying these things if we want to. It is characteristic of impersonal, abstracted talk about facts that these things are insinuated rather than mentioned, there being a world of difference, as any gossip knows, between insinuating and mentioning. The reason why 'fact' is defined modally as something which *can* be established, and not categorically as something which *is* established, is that in stating something to be a fact we abstract from the means of explaining or establishing it, and the price we pay for the privilege of abstracting is that we are always accountable for the facts. When several methods of verifying that something is a fact are on a par with one another, there is no reason to prefer one method rather than another: what is all-important is that the claim that it is a fact *could* be made good by giving a method for establishing it if taken to task.

Taine's maxim for historians, 'Après la collection des faits, la recherche des causes', has long seemed absurd to philosophers of history. Absurd it certainly is, for it amounts to saying 'After collecting those items which can be established, look for ways of establishing them.' If Taine were a squirrel he might have said, 'After hoarding those nuts which will last through the winter, look for ways of finding them', not of finding them again, albeit this be the epitome of squirrelhood, but of finding them in the first place. When an historian has a hunch concerning what can be established, he already has a rudimentary idea of how to go about establishing it; and when he knows what can be established he knows how to establish it. Thus Collingwood not without insight parried Taine with the aphorism that when the historian knows what happened, he also knows why it happened.

Events as well as facts can be established. Events as well as facts can be explained. The same goes for theoretical entities, scientific laws containing those entities, and the theories which sustain them; theorems within axiomatic systems and the systems which sustain them; not to mention such foggy items in the weather-charts of history as winds of doctrine, climates of belief, undercurrents of opinion and storms in teacups. The list could be expanded indefinitely, but enough has been said to raise the question once again: Facts, events, or neither one nor t'other? While it is of the meaning of 'fact' that a fact can be established or explained, there are many other kinds of thing which, as it happens, *can* be established or explained. Of these, those which can be designated by noun clauses are candidates for facthood. Significantly, 'establish' and 'explain' enter more than one battery. Some things which can be established, e.g. sites, cannot be explained, although one might explain why a battle was fought in one place rather than another; and other things, e.g. rainbows and mirages, are readily explained but seldom established. Is it so surprising that 'fact', 'event' and 'cause' enter more than one battery when such close verbal associates as 'establish' and 'explain' enter a multiplicity?

The quest for the logical structure of facts was misguided from the beginning. Facts and events, unlike propositions, are not the kinds of thing which exhibit logical structure. It all began with the mistaken assumption that a fact is a true proposition, which bye the bye has logical structure because it is a proposition, not because it is true. Since facts, alias true propositions, were thought to have their own logical structure, two other candidates for logical structure presented themselves by way of contrast, false propositions and events. And since propositions both true and false are intensional, events, so the argument runs, must be extensional. Richard Martin and Donald Davidson are in basic agreement on this, except that the one seeks to handle events as well as facts virtually and the other pirouettes on propositional attitudes. What about false propositions? Martin recognizes the intensional character of facts and seeks to avoid the embarrassment of false propositions by making facts nominal entities, fact-talk being through-and-through meta-linguistic. In treating facts as the referents of sentences Davidson seeks another escape, with a terminus equally ersatz. Parodying Church's parody of Frege, he presents us with quarrelsome twins, Fact and Anti-fact. I protest.

But whoa: my little buggy has gone far enough, having passed a narrow way in the going.

COMMENT

WESLEY C. SALMON

While I am in sympathy with Professor Martin's attempt to clarify the concept of an event, and with many features of the method he employs, there is one aspect of his discussion that troubles me. To state the matter concisely: the use of times in the construction of events is an extremely dubious procedure. This doubt arises, to be sure, from certain physical considerations, and Martin makes it quite clear that he is not attempting a reconstruction of the language of modern physics. 'Greater sophistication in the handling of time would no doubt be required,' he admits, 'if we were to consider more closely the actual language of physics.' Nevertheless, he goes on to say, 'It is not clear that this would require any fundamental change . . .' I am convinced, on the contrary, that the relevant physical considerations are of an extremely fundamental sort, and they have a direct bearing upon the explication of any really basic concept such as *event*. They demand a significant change in the approach if an adequate language for physics is to be developed. I should like to suggest, moreover, that these physical considerations have great relevance for attempts to clarify ordinary discourse about time and events, and they cannot be ignored when it comes to metaphysical judgments about the fundamental constituents of the world.

There is no question about the formal convenience that results from the supposition that a temporal or spatio-temporal manifold is available ready-made for use in constructing languages for various purposes. Carnap's use of 'co-ordinate languages' has made it quite apparent. Special relativity, however, focuses attention sharply upon the status of space and time, and upon their relations to the events and things that constitute physical reality. No longer can space and time be regarded as physical or metaphysical entities which enjoy independent existence as containers in which things and events are to be found. The basic reality seems, rather, to be a manifold of events (and possibly things) which bear causal relations to one another. The possibility or impossibility of a causal connection between two events is *the* basic factor determining the spatio-temporal relations between them. Einstein made this clear in his original paper on special relativity, and it has subsequently been elaborated by a large number of authors (especially Grünbaum and Reichenbach). Space and time are thus regarded as elaborate constructions based upon the causal relations among events. In order even to begin laying the foundations for the language of space and time, we must have already available the concept of an event as well as the concept of a causal process (such as the transmission of light).

Martin evidently feels there is nothing question-begging in his use of times as constituents of events. He is quite willing to quantify over time variables, and he allows them to flank the identity sign. Times are supposed to exist, and they are taken along with objects to construct events. They can be individuated and identified. The problem begins to emerge, when we realize that the identification of a time t_1 belonging to one event with a time t_2 belonging to another event involves the concept of simultaneity, which is, according to special relativity, dependent upon the existence of events and their causal nonconnectibility. Moreover, even the simple topological considerations Martin mentions are not straightforward. Whether the temporal manifold is one-dimensional or multi-dimensional, closed or open, bounded or unbounded—whether it is a linear continuum, cyclic, looped, etc. —depends upon the identity or nonidentity of events. The supposition that we can have even a very elementary time-language without a prior event-language is highly questionable.

Special relativity, with its close attention to space and time, has shown that the apparently clear-cut distinction between them is not as straightforward as we might have supposed. It appears likely, in consequence, that any attempt to adapt Martin's approach to the basic needs of physics would require that his purely temporal symbol 't' be replaced by a spatio-temporal one. I do not think this fact creates any additional problems for Martin's programme; indeed it might suggest a way of mitigating some of the foregoing difficulties. If one were willing to regard very limited space-time regions as the sort of thing that can be ostensive in character—that can simply be pointed out, without supposing that they fit together into a manifold with any particular kind of topological or metrical structure—then it might be possible to carry out a construction of events somewhat along the lines Martin is suggesting. I think it is much more reasonable, however, to regard spatio-temporal or causal coincidences, such as collisions, as the most fundamental ostensive objects, and these seem to qualify as events. Our current knowledge of space and time strongly suggests that the basic language of physics needs an explication of *event*, and of *causal process*, in nontemporal terms. Such explications would be extremely fruitful contributions to the philosophy of physics and to our ordinary understanding of the relations between events and time.

REPLY

R. M. MARTIN

First of all, I should like to thank both symposiasts for their perceptive comments. The points raised are important for our proper understanding of 'fact' and 'event', and after I have had my little further say, much will still remain to be clarified.

I

Davidson uses 'singular term' and 'complex singular term' without qualms to include such phrases as 'Caesar's death' as well as 'the cat', 'mange', 'Jack', 'Caesar', etc. But an enormous difference is glossed over here, namely, between those terms, singular or complex, which 'refer to' a clear-cut physical object (or perhaps even an abstract one) as over and against those which 'refer to' events in some unanalyzed sense. Concerning singular and complex terms referring to physical and perhaps abstract objects we have a well-developed syntax, and indeed semantics as well. Concerning 'terms' referring to events we have pitiably little syntax, and scarcely any semantics at all. Thus Davidson's very first paragraph asks us to presuppose more than we can, even with the most charitable will. We cannot presuppose the very syntax and semantics we are seeking to become clear about. Davidson wisely resists contending that true declarative sentences somehow 'correspond to' the facts. He is no 'devoted friend of facts', his devotion being poured out to events instead.

Davidson thinks that I have conflated two problems concerning 'facts', have neglected one of them, and 'mistakenly' think that 'sentences may be viewed as ersatz facts'. The problem neglected is the analysis of the basic idiom.

(1) The sentence 'The cat has mange' corresponds to the fact that the cat has mange.

'To establish the general dispensability of facts,' Davidson writes, 'Martin should deal with the singular term "the fact that the cat has mange" in (1).' Here are we again with Davidson's overpopulated realm of unanalyzed singular terms. Also 'corresponds to' in (1) has no precise meaning. The friends of facts have not given it one. Hence it is not clear why I or anyone 'should' do what Davidson says. Even so, I think a precise meaning for 'corresponds to' is forthcoming from the definition, in my paper 'Facts', of 'so-and-so-is-a-fact'. We can say, namely, that

The fact $\langle a, x\ni(\text{---}x\text{---})\rangle$ corresponds to the sentence c if and only if there are expressions a and b such that (etc.) and c is the result of writing b followed by a.

This, together with the semantical truth-predicate presupposed here along with its Adequacy Condition ('Tarski's paradigm' according to Quine), gives presumably all that is needed for correspondence-talk between sentences and facts. If the 'friends of facts' want more, it is by no means clear just what. Let them spell it out explicitly.

That Davidson fails here, along with most, to take into account the semantical truth-predicate together with its Adequacy Condition, is suggested by his first footnote. 'For simplicity's sake I speak as if truth were a property of sentences: *more properly* [italics mine] *it is a relation between a sentence, a person and a time.*' But basically this is precisely what truth is not. To be sure, there are important triadic relations with their three arguments a sentence, a person, and a time. Especially useful here is the pragmatical relation of *acceptance*. Using this, we may say that a person X accepts or *takes-as-true* a sentence a (of L) at time t. Presumably this relation is the fundamental one of a certain (narrow) part of pragmatics.[1] But it is a relation very different from the semantical truth-property and plays a very different role in philosophic analysis.

Let us get back now to the 'mistaken' view attributed to me,

---

[1] Cf. the author's 'Toward a Systematic Pragmatics' (*Studies in Logic and the Foundations of Mathematics*, Amsterdam: North-Holland Publishing Co., 1959).

that 'sentences may be viewed as ersatz facts'. The view is rather that facts are in some sense semantical constructs out of factual sentences. Davidson fails to note apparently that they are *semantical* constructs. We start out with the usual extensional or denotational semantics, build up truth and L-truth and hence L-semantics generally, and then find therein a 'model' for facts. Davidson confesses (in footnote 4) that he does 'not understand how the apparatus of virtual classes and relations helps' my analysis. But the use of such classes and relations is rather fundamental in the semantics presupposed. Davidson says, continuing in the same footnote, that I 'need singular terms referring to expressions [*structural descriptions*, presumably], and once the subject is an expression and not its reference' he does not 'see how it matters, for present concerns, whether the expression has one or another of various logically equivalent forms'. This is surely confused. Are virtual class expressions supposed to be 'logically equivalent' to expressions for real classes? And does he here suppose that we are concerned only with expressions, and not with their reference also? The discussion of facts takes place within a suitable semantics involving both. Davidson, along with most previous writers on the subject, has apparently failed to grasp here the full semantics needed for the analysis of facts.

Davidson thinks that further differences between him and me would emerge if we were to go on to discuss the so-called 'propositional attitudes'. Perhaps so. Propositions themselves need an analysis in terms of a general theory of intensions,[2] but a discussion of this would lead us afield.

II

Let us go on now to events. Davidson seems to say mistakenly that I deny that there are such things, for, 'unlike Martin', he writes, 'I do not see how to interpret some of our plainest language without supposing there are events.' Nor do I. The question is not whether there are such things, but what it is that they are. An *analysis* of them, or some *theory* about them, is what we wish. This I attempt to supply, Davidson does not.

Davidson thinks it correct to say that Leopold's meeting with

---

[2] See 'An Improvement in the Theory of Intensions', *Philosophical Studies*, 18 (1967); 33–38; 'On Objective Intensions and the Law of Inverse Variation', to appear; and 'On Proper Names and Frege's *Darstellungsweise*', *The Monist*, 51 (1967); 1–8. Also, *Belief, Intension, and Ontology*, in preparation.

Stephen on Bloomsday is identical with Leopold's meeting with Stephen on June 16, 1904. But 'not every encounter is a meeting' and on my account, Davidson says, 'no meeting is identical with an encounter, though between the same individuals and at the same time. Indeed, Leopold's first meeting with Stephen on Bloomsday *in Dublin* [italics added] cannot be identical with Leopold's first meeting with Stephen on Bloomsday. No stabbing [on my account] can be a killing and no killing can be a murder, no arm raising a signalling, and no birthday party a celebration. I protest.' And so indeed do I.

Two quite separate problems are raised here. One involves the insertion of the phrase 'in Dublin', and this we shall deal with in due course. The other is that on my account no stabbing can be a killing, etc. Consider the event $\langle b, S, c, t \rangle^e$ of Brutus, b, stabbing, S, Caesar, c, at time t. Was this event also the *same* event as Brutus' *killing*, K, of Caesar at t? Thus, should

(2) $\qquad \langle b, S, c, t \rangle^e \mathrel{\dot{=}} \langle b, K, c, t \rangle^e$

hold? (The '$\dot{=}$' is identity between ordered virtual n-tuples, with certain kinds of which events, it will be recalled, are identified.) Or are these rather distinct, but simultaneous, events involving the same persons? Davidson apparently thinks they are the same event. I should prefer to say that they are distinct but simultaneous events involving the same persons. But some stabbings can still be killings, on the existence assumption that

$\qquad (EX)(Ey)(Ez)(Ew)(X \, S \, y, z \, . \, X \, K \, y, z)$.

Surely nothing in my analysis prevents this. And the event of Brutus' both stabbing and killing Caesar at t is merely

(3) $\qquad\qquad \langle b, (S \frown K), c, t \rangle^e$,

where the relevant action is the *logical product* of stabbing and killing. Perhaps the stabbing is a *part* of the killing.

In a fuller account of the theory of events *via* virtual (or even real, if one wishes) ordered n-tuples, a good deal should be said as to how complex events are built up out of simple ones. And just what are the simple ones and how do we determine them? The simple events presumably arise only from the primitive predicates of the language at hand. And even here, perhaps only some primitive predicates, not all, give rise to events. Action-properties and -relations surely do, but whether qualities do is less clear. Also we form complex events out of simpler ones in various ways. Broad's motor accident discussed in my paper is an example

of a kind of a *successive* product. But there are also *simultaneous* products, such as that involved in (3), which may also be written
$$(\langle b, S, c, t\rangle^e \frown \langle b, K, c, t\rangle^e).$$
And in the case of any products, the constituent events are in some sense 'parts' of it. Thus the event going on in the motor accident during t_2 is a 'part' of the whole accident. So here, Brutus' stabbing of Caesar at t is a part of the complex event of his both stabbing and killing Caesar at t.

Another example which my account is not supposed to be able to accommodate is the event-description 'John's kissing a girl at precisely noon'. This is not unique, Davidson says, if John kissed two girls simultaneously. Suppose John kissed Alice and Bertha simultaneously at noon. The complex event, symbolized in obvious fashion (K kisses, not kills, but some kissings might be killings!), as
$$(\langle j, K, a, noon\rangle^e \frown \langle j, K, b, noon\rangle^e),$$
contains both constituent events as parts. So far, so good. One event here, the complex event described, and a very different event from either of its constituents, but unique just as each constituent is. Strictly 'John's kissing a girl at noon' is a very different event-description, but it is not clear that Davidson is asking for *its* analysis. Using the selection-operator, where (ϵx. Gx) is some selected girl, we would have here something like
$$\langle j, K, (\epsilon x. Gx), noon\rangle^e.$$
But Davidson is surely not here inviting us to dwell upon the technicalities of descriptive and selective functions.

III

The next 'mistake' I am supposed to have made involves the uniqueness of time. More of course needs to be said about this than was possible in my paper above. To assure that a property-event-description describes one and only one event, we must be sure that '*Gyt*' is taken to express either that y has G throughout the entire time t or that y has G during just one (consecutive) part of t. If Vesuvius erupts during the entirety of A.D. 79, then 'the eruption of Vesuvius in A.D. 79' is a unique event-description. And similarly if Vesuvius erupts during some consecutive part of that year and at no other parts. Caesar's death took place throughout some time-span t but at no proper part of t. Just how long did it take Caesar to die? Perhaps only a short time. Rasputin's death took longer. No matter. 'Caesar's death at t' describes an event uniquely provided Caesar was dying during the whole of t. But where t_1 is a proper part of t and even though Caesar was a-dying at t_1, 'Caesar's death at t_1', does not describe an event.

Strictly, we should be very clear here as to how 'Gyt' is interpreted. Without going too deeply into the matter, we note merely that the following seems to hold, in a great many cases if not all: namely, Gyt if and only if (i) y has G continuously throughout t (i.e., at every part, proper or not, of t), or (ii) y has G at one and only one proper consecutive part of t, or (iii) y has G at t but at no proper part of t. Of this, more anon elsewhere.

IV

Davidson says that 'Martin is dubious that Ramsey's claim that "Caesar died" must, or perhaps even can, be construed as asserting the existence of an event of a certain sort'. This is not quite correct. My comment was merely that Ramsey had not given an exact *analysis* of such phrases, a logic for them, as it were. If an event-ontology is to be presupposed, we need a whole *theory* about it, and presumably some relativity and quantum theory as well, and not just a few phrases assuring us of the 'existence of events of a certain sort'.

Now Davidson goes along with Ramsey in postulating in effect that there are events *sui generis* over which variables and quantifiers are to be admitted straightaway. This in itself is not objectionable, but it poses difficult problems of analysis and subsequent construction.

One of Davidson's main reasons for admitting events *sui generis* is in connection with the logic of action-sentences, and more particularly, with the presence of *adverbs* in such sentences.[3] Such admission helps solve a problem which, according to Davidson, is 'simple, and ubiquitous. It can be illustrated by pointing out that "Brutus stabbed Caesar in the back in the Forum with a knife" entails "Brutus stabbed Caesar in the back in the Forum" and both of these entail "Brutus stabbed Caesar in the back" and all of these entail "Brutus stabbed Caesar"; and yet our common

---

[3] See his 'The Logical Form of Action Sentences', in *The Logic of Action*, edited by Nicholas Rescher, Pittsburgh, 1967.

way of symbolizing these sentences reveals no logical connection.' This cannot be solved, Davidson thinks, by taking 'stabs' or 'stabbed' as an n-adic predicate, for we should have to know in advance a value for 'n' 'large enough to accommodate all eventualities'. This is the problem of 'variable polyadicity' and hinges in general on the problem of how to handle adverbs and prepositional phrases. Davidson thinks that this problem 'is solved by admitting events, and . . . has no other solution that . . . [he knows] of.' We wish now to offer some objections to his method and to suggest an alternative.

We can best approach Davidson's method by considering his simpler example, namely,

(4) 'I flew my spaceship to the Morning Star.'

This becomes for him, where 'x' now is a variable ranging over events in general,

(5) '(Ex)(Flew (I, my spaceship, x) . To (the Morning Star, x))'.

Here 'Flew' is a three-place predicate, the third argument of which is an event, and 'To' is a two-place predicate, the second argument of which is an event. Now

'Flew (I, my spaceship, x)'

presumably is to express that x is a flying-event, as it were, involving me and my spaceship.

'To (the Evening Star, x)'

expresses that x is a To-event, as it were, involving the evening star.

It is not necessary, Davidson says, 'to separate off the To-relation: instead we could have taken Flew as a four-place predicate'. But Davidson thinks it 'a merit of [his] . . . proposal that it suggests a way of treating prepositions as contributing structure'. Now structure is what we want, and this much is surely to the good. 'Not only is it nice to have the inference from (4) to . . .

(6) "(Ex) Flew (I, my spaceship, x)";

it is also nice to be able to keep track of the common element in 'fly to' and 'fly away from' and this of course we cannot do if we treat these as unstructured predicates.' Again, surely no predicate should be treated as 'unstructured'. But that treating prepositions in the way suggested contributes to structure seems doubtful. For one thing, Davidsonian relations such as To, Away From, perhaps With, Of, etc., remain rather murky affairs. At best we need to be told a good deal more about them than it seems we are. What is *their* structure?

Also an inference to something like (6) from (4) *can* surely be arranged, taking 'Flew' as a four-place predicate, i.e., with fixed polyadicity. Thus surely

(7)   'I flew my spaceship somewhere'

which is presumably inferable from (4) by a law of logic just as (6) is. In fact (6) might be thought to be mere ellipsis for (7). Also 'away from' and 'to' ought somehow to be definable in terms of vectors, or coordinates, or something of the kind, so that the 'common element' in 'fly to' and 'fly away from' need not be lost.

Davidson would no doubt agree with this in the case of predicates with fixed polyadicity. In ordinary language, however, we can add adverbial clauses *ad libitum*. But if the predicate involved is of fixed polyadicity, it is not clear how additional arguments can be added. The point seems well taken and more will be said about it in a moment.

Davidson does not give us any analysis of the *internal* structure of his events. They remain for him, it is to be feared, 'unstructured'. Surely structure is what we are trying to find almost always in logical analysis. Further the structure is there and if we fail to locate it something is amiss in our method.

Davidson notes that predicates other than action predicates have 'event-places' or events or arguments. 'Indeed,' he writes, 'the problems we have been mainly concerned with are not at all unique to talk of actions: they are common to talk of events of any kind'. An eclipse of the Morning Star is an eclipse of the Evening Star. Do we handle this, by parity of method, as

(8)   '(Ex) (Eclipse (x) . Of (Morning Star, x) . Of (Evening Star, x))'.?

It is not the concern over the identity of events that need worry us here, but rather the use of 'Of'. If we are not careful, we could make too much of 'Of'. Why not handle 'Cain is a brother of Abel' as

'(Ex) (Brother (Cain, x) . Of (Abel, x))',

where 'x' now ranges over physical objects? After all 'of' occurs in 'Cain is the brother of Abel' and it would be 'nice' to bring out the common structure in the two uses of 'of' in this and in 'An eclipse of the Morning Star is an eclipse of the Evening Star'. It is not clear that Davidson would go quite so far as this. The brakes would perhaps have to be put on at some point. But just where? And just why there? . . . Better not to need the brakes at all.

Also, without proper braking, it might appear that Davidson could dispense with all relations except prepositional ones. Thus rather than to take S or K dyadically, we take them as properties of events. 'S(x)' reads now 'x is a stabbing'. 'Brutus stabbed Caesar' could become

'(Ex)(S(x) . Of(x, Caesar) . By(x, Brutus))'

and so on. If we are not careful we will deplete the realm of relations (even virtual ones) excessively, therewith depriving mathematics and science of rather important and useful entities.

The 'Fido'-Fido principle, so-called and disparaged by Ryle, requires that to every word of a language there corresponds something or other which it designates. Perhaps no one now takes this principle seriously, unless suitably restricted. According to it, to prepositions there are some corresponding objects, perhaps the Davidsonian relations To, From, etc. Davidson does not explicitly invoke the discredited 'Fido'-Fido principle, but his recognition of prepositional relations is surely uncomfortably in accord with it.

There is also a perhaps dangerous increase in ontology, and hence in ontic commitment, with the new sort of variables over events. The problem remains for Davidson of showing us precisely how this new ontology is related to the one of physical objects. This latter ontology he admits anyhow. Any increase in ontology is in some sense dangerous, unless shown to be otherwise. There is the danger of admitting more than is needed. There is the danger of introducing obscure entities. And always concerning such there are additional non-logical postulates needed to characterize them and to interrelate them with entities already available.

Davidson worries about the criteria for individuating events in his sense. And well he may. But '. . . this must wait', he says. Quine's dictum, No identity, no ontology, is relevant here, so that the matter cannot wait at all. We simply do not know what Davidson's ontology is until he has given his criteria for identity and individuation. Meanwhile he cannot claim even remotely to have shown that 'the presumption lies with events' if taken as unanalyzed entities *sui generis*.

V

The problem of how to handle adverbs and prepositional phrases remains, if we eschew Davidson's strange relations To,

From, With, etc. A sketch of a theory of action was put forward in my 'Performance, Purpose, and Permission'.[4] Some suggestions there may perhaps guide us here. Let

'X Prfm f, x, t'

express that person X performs an action of type f on x at t. E.g., Brutus performs an action of the type stabbing on Caesar at time t. Strictly of course the action-type here is merely the dyadic relation of stabbing with the time explicitly brought in as an additional argument.

Some action-types are monadic, some dyadic, some perhaps triadic. Perhaps there are some quadratic ones also, but many of these can be introduced in terms of action-types of lower degree. There is no question of 'variable polyadicity' here any more than there is for the relation of being father of, the positive square root of, or being jealous of because of y's affection for z, and so on. Each action-type has its degree fixed once and for all, and in practice we probably never need primitively action-types of degree greater than three or four.

Action-types can be modified in various ways by appending adverbs and prepositional phrases. Usually these are in answer to such questions as How? Where? Whence? Whither? With what? etc. Given any action-type we can always find another one with an additional argument enabling us to answer one of these questions. Thus we not only have stabs (dyadically), but stabs with such and such an instrument (triadically), stabs in such and such at part of the body (triadically), stabs at such a place (triadically), and so on. We need not assume that only one additional argument will always be needed. For some cases two or more might be. No matter. We can always find additional action-types of fixed polyadicity to accommodate the additional adverbial clause.

If these suggestions are sound, 'Brutus stabbed Caesar at time t in the back in the Forum with a knife' becomes 'Brutus stabbed Caesar at time t, and Brutus stabbed Caesar at time t in the back, and Brutus stabbed Caesar at t in the Forum, and Brutus stabbed Caesar at t with a knife'. And similarly for any additional adverbial phrases one might wish to add.

These suggestions are not to be taken as supplying a full theory of the logical behaviour of adverbs, any more than David-

[4] *Philosophy of Science* 30 (1963), pp. 122–137.

sons's are. But they may well go a long way. And they enable us to dispense with Davidson's strange bedfellows To, With, etc., as well as with his unanalyzed events *sui generis* in the theory of action.

VI

It is true, as Professor Butler points out, that of a crucial definition, that of objective analytic intension, in Chapter V of *Intension and Decision*,[5] we tarried not the cooling and chanced to burn our lips. This does not entail, however, as Professor Butler comes close to suggesting, that the programme of building up intensions within a purely denotational or extensional semantics must be abandoned or is impossible to fulfillment. The fault here is in us, not in our stars. In fact, remedial measures were immediately suggested in three papers (referred to in footnote 2) along, we might say, somewhat Aristotelian lines. And in a fourth paper, remedial suggestions are made along the more Platonic lines of *Intension and Decision* itself.[6] They say that every mind is fundamentally either Platonic or Aristotelian, so that here one can take one's pick. Nothing in the paper on facts and events, however, hinges, Professor Butler curiously to the contrary, upon the adequacy or inadequcy of the theory of intensions in *Intension and Decision*.

Indeed it is 'futile' to 'idolize' either facts or events. Davidson idolizes events, but (happily) regards them as extensional entities. Butler idolizes both facts and events, (unhappily) regarding both as intensional. The chief danger of intensionalism is just this, that one idolizes intensions without subjecting them to the rough weather of clear dissection and analysis. What intensions are, if taken seriously and *sui generis*, no one has told us, above all, not Frege, Carnap, or Church. Nor have Professor Butler and his resolute Oxford lay brethren.

To do full justice to Professor Butler's comments would require a comparison of two rather different ways of doing philosophy and would end up with a plea for bridges between the two. Instead we must be content with a few rough remarks.

Butler seriously misrepresents my view, however, when he says in effect that my method is 'to foist upon a member of . . .

---

[5] Englewood Cliffs, N. J.: Prentice-Hall, 1963.
[6] See 'On Abstract Entities in Semantic Analysis', forthcoming in *Noûs*.

[a] family of interrelated concepts a preconceived theory' about facts and events. In the first place, there is no foisting, and in the second, no preconceived theory. The theory is designed *ad hoc* rather to fix fundamental, paradigmatic even, or 'core', meanings in what is hoped to be a satisfactory way theoretically. If we succeed in this, which is by no means easy, we can then study interconnections of the 'core' meaning with other members of the family. But there is no foisting, for we are free to alter the core should it not prove fruitful.

We must be careful not to confuse intensions (with an 's') with intentions (with a 't'). Professor Butler thinks that there are such things as 'intensional [with an 's'] happenings' and he registers here 'a plea for mental events', presumably the intentional (with a 't') entitles *par excellence*. Intensions (with an 's') on my view are purely semantical, whereas intentions (with a 't') seem best handled in terms of suitable epistemic or pragmatic relations. There may well be no intentional 'entities' but only the suitable relations.[7] However this may be, Professor Butler's remarks have not furthered our understanding of the delicate interrelationship between intensionality and intentionality.

The phrase 'in the event that' may well be, in certain occurrences at least, 'paraphrased' or 'transformed' into 'if'. 'In the event that you decide . . .' becomes 'If you decide . . .' 'In any event I shall ask you . . .' becomes 'If (periphrastically) no matter what event occurs, I shall ask you . . .' or 'For all events E, if E occurs then I shall ask you . . . .' To read more into the phrase 'in the event that', as Butler seems to do, is like reading a realm of *sakes* into Quine's 'for the sake of'. Of course there are multifoliate batteries of uses of terms. Our task, and of this Professor Butler apparently approves, is to arrive at a 'core meaning' and by this hopefully to be able to illuminate other usages, by way both of similarities and contrasts.

On one point it seems to me that Butler misreads Ramsey. Ramsey does *not* say that 'the death of Caesar' 'names' a fact. It can be 'used in two different ways', Ramsey says (p. 141 of 'Facts and Propositions'), as a 'description of an event' or 'in a context like "He was aware of the death of Caesar" meaning "He was aware that Caesar had died".' In this latter case, Ramsey thinks, the awareness is not of an event but of 'an event and a character

---

[7] Cf. *Belief, Intension and Ontology.*

also', the 'character' (if it be such) here presumably being that of having occurred. Butler's reading leaves out the crucial phrase 'and a character also'.

Butler thinks that 'events as well as facts can be established. Events as well as facts can be explained'. Nonetheless, he says, 'facts and events, unlike propositions, are not the kinds of things which exhibit logical structure'. This is an obscurantist view indeed. It is like saying that such and such a phenomenon in physics can be 'established and explained' but that this phenomenon is not the kind of thing that can exhibit physical structure. Clearly structure is what we wish to get at, in logical analysis as well as in scientific theory, and we shall never find anything that lacks it. Hence the scientific and philosophic quest for structure is unending. But the horse and buggy must be left behind, just as older physical theories must.

Symposium III

EXISTENCE-ASSUMPTIONS IN PRACTICAL THINKING

S. KÖRNER

Many people believe that at some times in their life they have an opportunity for 'effective choice', i.e. for different kinds of chosen bodily conduct which, on the one hand, are not predetermined by the past and, on the other, respectively predetermine different realizable futures. My chief aim in this paper is to examine the nature of the assumptions that the notion of effective choice is not empty, and that effective choices between alternative courses of action are occasionally made by human beings, in accordance with, or contravention of, their prudential or moral evaluations. In the first section I shall attempt an analysis of two concepts of effective choice, indicating their rôle in planning. In the next section I shall turn to the problem of 'practical existence'—of existence from the practical point of view—by briefly considering three types of a metaphysics of planning, as exemplified by Hume, Kant and Peirce. In the light of some lessons which can be learned from these philosophers, I shall outline, in the third section, a tentative justification of practical existence-assumptions. Since I am here trying to develop further certain ideas which I expressed in another essay,[1] some overlap between the two essays was unavoidable.

(i) *On some concepts employed in planning a course of action.* A person planning a course of action might well map it out in the form of a tree-diagram of which the following figure could be a part. (See overleaf.)
A capital Roman letter with or without a bar, e.g. B or $\bar{B}$, stands for a proposition to the effect that a spatio-temporally delimited situation (process, chain of events, etc.) possesses, or that it does not possess, a certain conjunction of characteristics, e.g. β. A small Roman letter with or without a bar, e.g. p or $\bar{p}$, stands for a

[1] 'On the Concept of the Practicable,' *Proc. Ar. Soc.*, 1966–67, pp. 1–16.

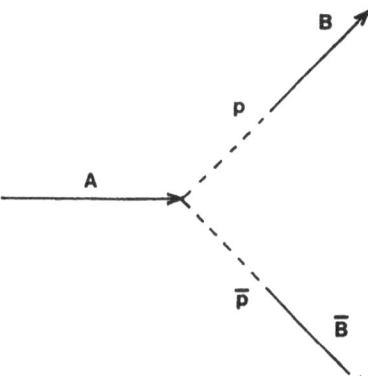

proposition that the planner's spatio-temporally delimited *chosen* bodily conduct possesses, or that it does not possess, a certain conjunction of characteristics, e.g. π. The terms 'chosen' and 'choice' refer to a familiar experience—in Hume's words[2] 'a seeming experience, which we have, or may have, of liberty or indifference in many of our actions'—without prejudging the question whether it is, as Hume holds, a 'false sensation'. By juxtaposing the Roman letters which separately abbreviate propositions describing situations or chosen bodily conduct, we form the abbreviation of a proposition which describes a sequence of these items. Thus Ap abbreviates a proposition describing a sequence in which the item described by A is immediately followed by the item described by p; and $A \ldots B$ abbreviates the description of a sequence in which the two specified items are separated by one or more unspecified ones. The diagram without the arrowheads maps the courses of action which the planner regards as practicable, i.e. as effectively choosable by him. The route marked by the arrowheads is the course of action he proposes to take. The detailed construction of the diagram depends on the planner's empirical beliefs, on his general practical belief that the course of nature allows for effective choices, and on his methods for determining his opportunities for effective choices.[3] The selected route depends on his personal aims, moral convictions and his methods for evaluating practicabilities in accordance with them.

[2] *Enquiry Concerning Human Understanding*, p. 94 (Selby-Bigge edition, Oxford 1902 etc.)
[3] (Added after symposium) I use 'effective choice' as an abbreviation of 'effectively chosen bodily conduct'.

A planner's judgments as to what is practicable—as to how he can influence the course of nature by effective choices—presuppose that he has a conception of the course of nature as uninfluenced by the interference of his effective choices. He must in particular employ at least one predictive concept, i.e. a relation between propositions which licenses predictive inferences from one proposition describing a situation, bodily conduct or a sequence of such items to another such proposition. As examples of predictive concepts, I shall, without further analysis, use a concept of empirical necessitation, briefly *emp*, belonging to the Hume-Kant-Mill family of causal relations; and a concept of empirical probabilification, briefly *prob*, which unlike the classical concept of probability, is not definable as imperfect knowledge of empirical necessitations. To simplify the discussion, I shall assume that a planner uses only one of these concepts. If he uses another predictive concept, or more than one, certain more or less obvious modifications are required.

A planner who on the one hand uses *emp* as his only predictive concept and yet believes that the realization of his plans depends on the availability of effective choices must, in order to leave room for them, restrict the applicability of *emp*. Assume that, in accordance with our diagram, he is in the situation described by A and chooses, by bodily conduct as described by p, to bring about the situation described by B. I shall abbreviate the description of his particular choice, which may or may not be effective, by $Ch(Ap\ B)$. For the choice to be effective the following further conditions must be fulfilled[4]: (i) $\sim(A\ emp\ p)$ and $\sim(A\ emp\ \bar{p})$, where the absence of *emp* is not due to the situation's and the bodily conduct's being incompletely described by A and p. That is to say, neither p nor $\bar{p}$ are empirically necessitated by A, and the bodily conduct is not solely dependent on the situation or its predecessors. (ii) In the sequences $A \ldots B$ and $A \ldots \bar{B}$ neither B nor $\bar{B}$ are connected with A by one or more *emps*[5] (iii) $Ap\ emp\ B$ and $A\bar{p}\ emp\ \bar{B}$. If these conditions are satisfied, I shall say that Ap selectively necessitates B and $A\bar{p}$ selectively necessitates $\bar{B}$, briefly $Ap\ selemp\ B$ and $A\bar{p}\ selemp\ \bar{B}$. The choice described by $Ch(Ap\ B)$ is effective if $Ap\ selemp\ B$. The question whether the

[4] (Added after symposium) The conjunction of the conditions is necessary and sufficient.
[5] (Added after symposium) I.e. $\sim(A\ emp\ B)$, $\sim(A\ emp\ \bar{B})$ and there are no sequences $A\ldots B$ or $A\ldots\bar{B}$ which are linearly ordered by *emp*.

planner is justified in assuming that *selemp* is not empty and, if so, whether it applies in a given situation is for the moment left unanswered.

A planner who on the one hand uses *prob* as his only predictive concept and yet believes that the realization of his plans depends on the availability of effective choices, must in order to leave room for them, restrict the applicability of *prob*. It should be noted that an expression such as e.g. *A prob B* is elliptical in that it does not contain any indication of the degree to which *A* probabilifies *B* although the degree of probability is conceived as definite, or at least, as lying within certain definite limits. With this *proviso* we can define what is meant by effective choice if the only predictive concept is *prob*. The definition is analogous to the one given in the preceding paragraph. A choice described by *Ch(Ap B)* is effective if[6] (i) ~ (*A prob B*) and ~ (*A prob B̄*); (ii) in the sequences *A . . . B* and *A . . . B̄* neither *B* nor *B̄* are connected with *A* by one or more *prob*s; (iii) *Ap prob B* and *Ap̄ prob B̄*. If these conditions are satisfied, I shall say that *Ap* selectively probabilifies *B* and *Ap̄* selectively probabilifies *B̄*, briefly *Ap selprob B* and *Ap̄ selprob B̄*. The choice described by *Ch (Ap B)* is effective if *Ap selprob B*. The question whether the planner is justified in assuming that *selprob* is not empty and, if so, whether it applies in a given situation is again for the moment left unanswered.

The assumption that there are effective choices is central to all planning and thus adds a practical significance to both empirical and evaluative thinking which they otherwise would lack. The determination of practicabilities includes the determination of empirical possibilities and thus depends on empirical thinking; and a planner's evaluations of empirical possibilities presupposes that some of them are practicable. Planning is not just prediction, but prediction and evaluation of practicabilities. In adding practical significance to empirical thinking, the assumption that there are effective choices *ipso facto* adds practical significance to the employment of scientific theories. And in adding practical significance to evaluative thought, it *ipso facto* adds practical significance to evaluative theories which are related to commonsense evaluation in ways which are analogous to the relation which scientific theories bear to commonsense empirical thinking.

The relation between empirical thinking and its theoretical

---

[6] (Added after symposium) and only if

refinements has often been investigated.[7] The relation between commonsense evaluation and its theoretical refinements e.g. in welfare economics, the theory of games and decision-theory generally, has not to the same extent been made the subject of philosophical analysis. As a comparatively simple example of what is involved, one may consider a planner who is trying to evaluate practicabilities, defined in terms of *emp* and *selemp*, by ranking them in order of preference or indifference in accordance with his more or less clearly formulated conception of prudence and justice. One of the difficulties he is likely to meet has its root in the notions of evaluative indistinguishability or indifference which in general, like perceptual indistinguishability, is not transitive and of evaluative preference which in general is also not transitive. The conflict between his desire for an adequate evaluation of practicabilities and for manageable rules of inference may lead to the replacement of the original non-transitive by idealized transitive notions, with which they are in limited contexts identifiable. If the ranking is not merely individual but social, i.e. an aggregation of individual rankings, then the difficulties multiply and the need for simplification at the cost of some misrepresentation increases. Thus Arrow's impossibility theorem[8] shows that even very simple and apparently 'natural' conditions imposed on a highly idealized welfare-function are self-contradictory. These matters cannot be discussed here. My reason for mentioning them at all is simply to indicate how the practical significance of evaluative thinking, which rests on the assumption that the concept of effective choice is not empty, is transferred from commonsense evaluative thinking to its theoretical ramifications.

(ii) *Three representative metaphysical theories of planning.* An alleged effective choice, whether defined in terms of selective necessitation or selective probabilification, may turn out to be ineffective by the discovery of a hitherto unknown non-selective necessitation or probabilification. On the other hand, with the emergence of new possibilities of choice, the class of alleged effective choices may become larger. However, neither the contraction nor the expansion of this class implies that the concept of effective choice is or is not empty. The question is empirically undecidable. This was clear to Hume, Kant and Peirce from

---

[7] See e.g. *Experience and Theory* (London, 1966).
[8] *Social Choice and Individual Values* (London, 1951), Chapter V.

whose different answers some lessons can be learned about the nature of the question.

'Liberty,' says Hume, 'when opposed to necessity, not to constraint, is the same thing with chance; which is universally allowed to have no existence.' (op. cit., p. 95) His reason for agreeing with this opinion, which nowadays is no longer universal, is that he regards the 'relation of *Cause and Effect*' as indispensable to all thinking since 'by means of this relation alone we can go beyond the evidence of our memory and senses.' (op. cit., p. 26) and since without its applicability and application not only the natural sciences, but also history, politics understood as a science and the 'foundation of *morals*' would be impossible. Hume's argument here foreshadows the Kantian transcendental deductions. He argues from the indispensability of the category of causality to himself, and to those who are imprisoned in the same categorial system, to its absolute indispensability—from the relatively to the absolutely conceivable and inconceivable. The argument would be fallacious even if one could not point to categorial systems, in which Hume's category of causality, has no place.[9]

Although Hume's principal argument is transcendental, in that it tries to answer the question how thinking about matters of fact *in general*, including scientific thinking, is possible, one may reasonably suspect that it is based on a metaphysical extrapolation and a misunderstanding of the science of his time. He extrapolates the determinism of Newton's physical theory to the universe as a whole and he does not recognise that the concepts of physics are not perceptual, although within limited contexts they are identifiable with perceptual concepts. Hume's remarks of the law of inertia illustrate both these mistakes (op. cit., p. 73 footnote).

If the relation of causality applies to all phenomena, then some apparently 'contradictory phenomena'—to use a Humean locution (op. cit., p. 20) . . . must be saved by reinterpretation. Of these two seem particularly important to Hume. First, 'we imagine we feel a liberty within ourselves' (op. cit., p. 94, footnote); second, in blaming vice and praising virtue, we seem to believe that vicious or virtuous actions have been effectively chosen and are not, like (unchosen) personal beauty or deformity, empirically necessitated (op. cit., p. 102). As regards the first apparently contradictory

[9] See 'Transcendental Tendencies in Recent Philosophy', *The Journal of Philosophy* 53, No. 19 (1966).

phenomenon, Hume shows how, if one accepts his well-known analysis of the concept of causal connection, the feeling of liberty within ourselves can be explained as an illusion. As regards the second, Hume requires us to assimilate moral to merely aesthetic praise or blame. If, as it must be, Hume's thesis is abandoned, i.e. if neither his concept of universal empirical necessitation nor any other predictive concept is indispensable, then the need for reinterpreting the feeling of liberty and for reinterpreting the belief that moral and aesthetic praise or blame differ radically, no longer arises; and they may be reinstated as *prima facie* evidence for the existence of effective choices.

Kant rejects Hume's or similar manoeuvres in reinterpreting moral feelings and beliefs as a 'miserable makeshift' and 'petty verbal hairsplitting'.[10] The question which he thinks answerable and which he tries to answer is: How are natural science *and* moral experience (conceived as including a true belief in the existence of effective choices) possible? He agrees with Hume's thesis that the only concept used in the prediction of matters of fact is the relation of cause and effect and also on the whole with Hume's phenomenological description of practical thinking. But he argues from a very different epistemological position: the indispensability of the concept of causality is based on the concept's being *a priori* in the sense that (i) it is not perceptual; (ii) that experience could not be objective without the applicability and application of the concept; and (iii) that the applicability of the concept and of the other categories implies the existence of a non-phenomenal world to which they are inapplicable and which is, therefore, not accessible to any thinking and perceiving being, since thinking and perceiving cannot proceed without their application. It is mainly in the third of these points that Kant and Hume differ radically from each other.

If we accept it, the statements that phenomena are subject to causality and that the noumenal world is not subject to it are compatible. It also follows that man as a noumenon is not subject to causality, although as a phenomenon he is. But the difficulties to which Kant's answer to his own question gives rise, are, as has often been pointed out, very great indeed. I shall mention only one: allegedly effective choices are made by individual men. Yet only phenomena are instances of the categories and have spatio-

[10] *Critique of Practical Reason* (edition of the Berlin Academy, p. 96).

temporal location, which is their principle of individuation. One can thus, as Schopenhauer pointed out, attach no clear meaning to an individuation of the noumenal world into separate noumenal individuals. A Kantian might, of course, argue that since his system of categories is uniquely associated with any thinking about matters of fact, effective choices are only possible, if the noumenal world consists of individuals and if every man is a noumenal individual. The argument piles one transcendental deduction upon another. It is, moreover, not only exposed to the general criticism which can be made of any transcendental deduction, but can also be refuted by counterexamples: orthodox quantum mechanics is associated with a categorial schema which does not comprise the Kantian concept of causality, as constitutive of objective experience.

Kant himself does not seem to have been entirely satisfied with his proof that the unrestricted applicability to phenomena of the concept of causality is compatible with the assumption that there are effective choices. In his doctrine of the 'primacy of pure practical reason in its connection with theoretical reason'[11] he argues that if speculative reason and practical reason were merely 'co-ordinated' there would arise 'a conflict of reason with itself'. Speculative reason, he therefore holds, must be subordinate to practical reason 'because all interests are in the last analysis practical' and 'even the interest of the speculative reason is merely conditional and complete only in its practical employment'. Although this doctrine is closely connected with Kant's transcendental idealism, it contains the germ of an independent justification of the assumption that the concept of effective choice—whether it be understood as selective necessitation or selective probabilification—is not empty.

Peirce rejects the doctrine of the indispensability of the Humean or Kantian concept of causality to thinking about matters of fact. He argues[12] that if one traces the causes of errors of observation back far enough, one will be 'forced to admit they are always due to arbitrary determination or chance'; and he recognizes that 'the determined advocate of exact regularity will soon find himself driven to *a priori* reasons to support his arguments'.

---

[11] *Critique of Practical Reason* (edition of the Berlin Academy, p. 119 ff.)
[12] 'The Doctrine of Necessity Re-examined' *Collected Papers*, ed. Hartshorne and Weiss (Harvard, 1931–35), Vol. 6.

Peirce's arguments are also *a priori*, resting as they do on a metaphysical interpretation of the theory of errors of observation; but his own replacement of the concept of empirical necessitation by a concept of probabilification, which requires the existence of irreducible chance in nature, does not imply that he has thereby abandoned scientific or commonsense thinking about matters of fact. The dispensability of the Humean or Kantian concept of causality in scientific thinking has been clearly borne out by the development of physics and may one day become a commonplace in very ordinary discourse. It is, moreover, important to emphasize that even though the concept of causality is for the purposes of science and commonsense thinking dispensable, it does by no means follow that the concept by which it is replaced is itself indispensable. There is no reason to assume that a return to the older categorial system is impossible. Indeed it may even be that one day predictively richer, logically simpler, and aesthetically more satisfying scientific and commonsense beliefs will be housed in the categorial system which Peirce has abandoned or in a categorial system so far unconceived by anybody.

Of itself the replacement of 'empirical necessitation' by 'empirical probabilification', as the only concept used in prediction, does not imply the existence of effective choices. But it allows for metaphysical manoeuvres which avoid the 'necessitarian' conclusion that 'our notion that we decide what we are going to do is reduced to illusion (loc. cit.)'. Peirce's anti-necessitarian metaphysics which conceives the world as a developing system subject to law, chance and 'habit-taking' does not, however, contain any clear and unambiguous answer to the problem whether, and if so in what sense, effective choices exist.[13]

From an examination of Hume's, Kant's and Peirce's doctrines of freedom and natural necessity a number of points become clearer. The failure of their transcendental arguments, to the effect that *any* predictive category is indispensable if prediction is to be possible at all, should make us distrust all arguments to the effect that, if a particular concept is successfully used in predictions, it follows that the concept of effective choice is (or that it is not) empty. From Hume's success in adjusting apparently unfavourable introspective evidence to his 'necessitarianism', we may learn not to put too much trust in introspective evidence.

[13] See e.g. W. B. Gallie, *Peirce and Pragmatism* (New York, 1966), p. 210.

Again from Kant's and Peirce's successes in making a reasonable case against necessitarianism, without revising the body of science which seems to suggest it, we may learn to distrust the relevance of metaphysical extrapolations to practical problems and their philosophical analysis. Lastly, from Kant's doctrine of the primacy of practical over speculative reason we may, after divesting it of its transcendentalism, take a useful hint for the solution of our problem.

(iii) *The existence of effective choices.* In defining two concepts of effective choice, namely selective empirical necessitation and probabilification, I have not prejudged the question of their emptiness or otherwise. As is agreed even by convinced fatalists, the *definientia*—the concepts of spatio-temporally delimited situations, of chosen bodily conduct, of (non-selective) necessitation or probabilification—are not empty. But non-emptiness of the *definientia* does not, of itself, imply non-emptiness of the *definiendum*. In this respect the concept of effective choice is similar to the concept of a unicorn. Both concepts are fashioned out of empirical or, at least empiricist, material. However, the existence of unicorns is empirically decidable in a way in which the existence of effective choices is not. The body of contemporary empirical knowledge implies that there are no unicorns. It does not, unless supplemented by metaphysical premises of the type discussed in the preceding section, imply either that there exist or that there do not exist effective choices.

The assumption that there are effective choices is made at every stage of planning: in discerning courses of action which are, at least with some degree of probability, practicable; in fitting such courses of action into a tree diagram of planning; in the prudential or moral evaluation of the branches and the routes made up from them; in the choice of one of these routes. Although empirically undecidable, the assumption can be justified from the practical point of view. The justification is quite simple and, substantially, quite ancient.

Every planner has the desire to reach a more or less clear goal. If, as I shall assume, his desire is serious, then it includes the desire not to miss any chance of an effective choice which brings his aim nearer to fulfilment. He may act on the positive assumption that there are effective choices or on the negative assumption that there are none. If the negative assumption is true, it is impossible for him to miss any; no chance can be missed where none exists. If the positive assumption is true, then he may miss a chance of a relevant effective choice by acting on the negative assumption; and he may avail himself of a chance which by acting on the negative assumption, he might miss. Thus if acting on one of the two assumptions serves the achievement of one's aims at all, then acting on the positive assumption serves it better. The argument justifies a planner in making the practical assumption that the concept of effective choice is not empty or, as one might say, that the concept of effective choice is not practically empty.

The argument rests on (a) an anthropological premiss, namely, that men are planners and desire not to miss the chances, if any, of achieving their aims, and (b) a prudential rule which is either characteristic of all planning or as a matter of fact accepted by all planners. One must be careful not to interpret practical non-emptiness too widely or too narrowly. It is in particular not empirical non-emptiness, since it is empirically undecidable. But it is not a mere practical fiction, which bids us to act *as if* an assumption were true which—like the useful assumption that all other drivers are drunk—we know from experience to be false. Again, the concept of effective choice must not be confused with the Kantian Idea of freedom. For the applicability of the concept, though not empirically verifiable, is in some cases, like *e.g.* hypnosis, at least empirically falsifiable. The applicability of the Idea, on the other hand, is empirically neither verifiable nor falsifiable. (To falsify the assumption that a concept is inapplicable to some situations is, of course, not to falsify the assumption of its applicability in general, i.e. to prove its emptiness.)

Every planner, *qua* planner, assumes—and is justified in assuming—that the concept of effective choice is practically not empty. The justification of the assumption that a particular choice is effective is a more complex matter. One reason for this is, as has been pointed out already, that the extension of the class of choices which are assumed to be effective is not constant, since with the increase of empirical knowledge some choices turn out to be ineffective, while hitherto impossible choices become possible and thus possibly effective. A planner will on the whole be justified in assuming the effectiveness of a choice, whose effectiveness is empirically undecidable. And the justification will follow the lines on which the assumption of the non-emptiness of the concept of effective choices was given its practical justification. However, some qualifications will be needed which take into account not only the planner's desire not to miss his chances, but also his desire not to take unreasonable risks of wasting his efforts.

In any case, however, if the planner is justified in assuming that the concept of effective choice is practically not empty, and if he desires to achieve his aims as nearly as possible, he will be well advised to acquire the empirical knowledge, including the scientific knowledge, on which at any time the demarcation of the class of empirically undecidable, but practically existent effective choices partly depends. Moreover, in the construction of a planning diagram one tries to determine not only opportunities for effective choices, but also the course of events which follows them without being open to deliberate interference. On the assumption, therefore, that effective choices exist, the planner's success depends on his general empirical knowledge. And acting on the assumption demands increase of empirical knowledge.

Again if effective choices exist and are relevant to the planner's aims, then their clear formulation in prudential or moral terms, and their prudential and moral ranking, is not a mere academic exercise. For, then, the planner's success is dependent on this clarification and ranking and, *if* the concept of moral knowledge is meaningful and not empty, on the increase of moral knowledge. Acting on the assumption that there are effective choices, demands not only the increase of empirical knowledge but the increase also of evaluative knowledge or, at least, of clarity in evaluative thinking. In this sense the primacy of practical over empirical and evaluative thinking, or, in a somewhat attenuated manner, of practical over theoretical reason, may be reasonably asserted.

At this point a determined determinist may object, that even if my argument was both non-metaphysical and correct, it still makes no sense of an effective choice. He might add that chosen bodily conduct which is not empirically necessitated or empirically probabilified by its spatio-temporal antecedents, is inconceivable except as a miracle; and that the determinist metaphysics, in spite of its reinterpretation of 'apparently contradictory phenomena', can at least do without miracles. But it is not at all difficult to oppose to the miracle-free determinist metaphysics an indeterminist metaphysics which is also miracle-free. For it does not follow at all that chosen bodily conduct which is not either empirically necessitated or probabilified, is therefore miraculous. It may, after all, within limits set by empirical necessitation or probabilification, be determined in an altogether different manner by entities which have no spatio-temporal location. Let me, partly following Frege,[14] sketch one such possibility.

The entities in question are Fregean 'thoughts', which exist independently of being apprehended, of being accepted as true or rejected as false, or of being communicated. They are without spatio-temporal location. 'Thoughts,' says Frege, 'are not wholly unreal although their reality is wholly different from the reality of things.' By being apprehended and accepted as true, they act on the course of nature, but their action—unlike the action of external upon external entities—is without interaction. To this peculiarity of the manner in which thoughts determine the deliberate interference of e.g. my body with the course of nature, another might be added, which Frege does not mention: if a thought in a situation determines me to act in one way rather than in another, this determination depends not only on the situation and on the thought, but also on myself. It is thus *I* who by suitable, effectively chosen, bodily conduct have some, however small, effect on the world and my effective choices are characteristic of myself in a way in which nothing else is.

I find nothing repellent in this speculation, which fits the practical assumption that there are effective choices to the introspected phenomena of choosing. However, no such speculation is needed to justify, from the practical point of view, the assumptions made by every planner: that the class of effective choices is not empty, that some particular choices are reasonably assumed to belong to it, and that its correct demarcation is best served by a continual improvement of empirical knowledge and evaluative clarity.

[14] 'Der Gedanke' reprinted in *Logische Untersuchungen*, ed. G. Patzig (Göttingen, 1966).

J. J. THOMSON

Professor Körner says that 'the assumption that there are effective choices is central to all planning'. I take it he means to be saying that a man who is making plans, or deliberating about what to do, assumes that his choice, whatever it is, will be an effective choice. But if I have not misunderstood his definition of the term 'effective choice' it seems to me that he is mistaken in this.

Körner gives two sets of defining conditions for the term 'effective choice', and it is not clear to me what he takes the relation between them to be. I shall concentrate only on the first set, since it seems to me that it is the first set, indeed the first member of the first set, which is most important to him.

Suppose a man is 'in the situation described by A and chooses, by bodily conduct as described by p, to bring about the situation described by B'; then his choice is an effective choice if and only if it meets three conditions. Condition (iii) is this: A and p together empirically necessitate B, and A and not-p together empirically necessitate not-B. His choice is effective only if it meets this condition; that is, only if his doing what p describes him as doing is, in A, empirically sufficient for B, and (as the second conjunct tells us) empirically necessary for B. Now the term 'effective choice' is a technical one, and Körner may define it as he wishes. But let us note that a great many choices which people make will fail to meet this condition, and hence turn out not to be effective choices. E.g., a night-watchman might wish to get revenge on his employer, and choose to leave the doors unlocked at night, in the hope that something valuable will be stolen. We may suppose that his leaving the doors unlocked is not, in the circumstances, empirically sufficient for getting something stolen. A burglar is needed too, and none may be forthcoming. Nor need we suppose the night-watchman even to think there is one forthcoming; he may have chosen to leave the doors unlocked in the mere hope that there will be one, and that something will be stolen. Again, Smith may choose to shoot Jones in order to kill him. We may suppose that shooting was not, in the circumstances, empirically necessary for the bringing about of Jones' death. Stabbing would have brought it about too, and Smith had a knife. We may suppose Smith to have known that stabbing would also have brought about Jones' death, but to have chosen to shoot Jones instead.

So there are choices which people make which will not count as effective choices. But mightn't people who make choices which are not effective choices be supposed to have deliberated about whether or not to make them? Surely the night-watchman might have deliberated about the risks to himself before deciding to leave the doors unlocked; surely Smith might have deliberated about whether to shoot or stab Jones. If so, there are people who on occasion plan and deliberate, but without supposing that their choice, whichever it is, will be an effective choice.

Körner might reply that I have misunderstood him. He might say that the two agents I described above did make choices which meet condition (iii), and that it only seemed they did not because of a misunderstanding of what is to be replaced for the variable B. B was to be replaced in a given case by a description of the situation a man who, in A, chooses to do p, is choosing to do p to bring about. So, in the second of the two cases I mentioned, I replaced B by 'Jones is killed'; then I said that Smith might choose to bring this situation about by shooting Jones, and that it might also be the case, and known to be the case by Smith, that shooting Jones was not empirically necessary for bringing it about. But Körner might say that if Smith does choose to shoot Jones where, e.g., stabbing would also have worked, and Smith knows this, then it must be supposed that Smith's end was not just to bring about Jones' being killed; if he chose shooting over stabbing where both were possible, and each would have worked, then it must be supposed he had a reason, as it might be, the neatness and tidiness of a shot—thus, that what he wanted was 'Jones is killed in the neatest and tidiest way', and not just 'Jones is killed'. For this, shooting was necessary. (How, after all, could Buridan's ass be said to *choose* the bale of hay on the right, if, by hypothesis, he does not want it, or anything about it, more than he wants the bale of hay on the left?)

Again, Körner might say that if the night-watchman (*really*) wanted something to be stolen, he wouldn't just leave the doors unlocked; he would arrange for the theft himself. So if all he does is leave the doors unlocked, then it must be supposed that all he really wanted was, not 'Something is stolen', but 'It is possible that (more likely that) something will get stolen.' For this, leaving the doors unlocked was sufficient. (After all, isn't *the* sign of wanting—*real* wanting—'trying to get'?)

If these moves are acceptable, then it will turn out that every (real) choice of a course of action will be a choice of an action which is empirically necessary and empirically sufficient for the situation the chooser wants to bring about. Are they acceptable? I think not. The second surely won't do; the first is more interesting, but (as I think) chiefly in that it is an interesting question why one feels so sympathetic towards it. But however interesting these questions may be, it seems to me that Körner is not really concerned with them in his paper. What interests and concerns him is not condition (iii) for 'effective choice', but rather condition (i).

Condition (i) says that a man's choice of bodily conduct p is effective only if it is *not* the case that A, his situation, empirically necessitates p or empirically necessitates not-p. Part of this seems clear. Suppose a man chooses to do p; but suppose that he cannot do it, his situation (which includes the state of his body) preventing him from doing it. E.g., a man might choose to raise his arm, and his arm be tied down, so that he cannot raise it. In such a case, the man's choice fails to meet condition (i). If we call the choice in such a case a 'non-actable' choice, then we could say that condition (i) says that a man's choice is effective only if it is actable. But from here on the rest is less clear. Suppose a man's choice to do p is an actable choice, and he actually does do p. His choice may still fail to meet condition (i), however: for it may be that his situation empirically necessitated that he do p. What I think Körner has in mind here is this. Suppose a man chooses to do p, and therefore does it. One kind of determinist might say that in every such case what happens is that the man's situation empirically necessitates his choosing to do p, this in the circumstances empirically necessitating his doing p. A second kind of determinist might say that in these cases what happens is that the man's situation empirically necessitates his choosing to do p and empirically necessitates his doing p, but does not necessitate the latter by necessitating the former—the choosing being (perhaps) a mere 'epiphenomenon'. Still a third kind of determinist might say that in these cases what happens is that our man's bodily situation necessitates his doing p, and something else necessitates his choosing to do p, these two going along quite independently, his choice to do p and what necessitates it being independent of what necessitates his doing p. And perhaps there are other kinds of determinists. If we suppose, as I take it Körner would wish us to suppose, that empirical necessitation is transitive, then they all have in common this: they all say that the agent's situation empirically necessitates his doing p. Körner's point here, then, is (as I take it): a man's choice to do p is effective only if the determinists I mentioned are mistaken about it. More generally, there are effective choices only if these determinists are wrong.

Condition (i) is thus a very different kettle of fish from condition (iii). Condition (iii) says that a man's choice is effective only if the *action* he chooses is in a certain sense effective, namely empirically necessary and sufficient for achieving his end. Condition (i) by contrast says that his choice is effective only if his *situation* is *not* effective in either of two ways: his situation must not necessitate that he does act on his choice, and his situation must not necessitate that he does not act on his choice.

That Körner is primarily interested in condition (i) comes out, I think, in his claim that the question whether or not there are any effective choices is 'empirically undecidable'. For the question whether or not there are any choices which meet condition (iii) is a quite straightforward question—if any question whether one thing is empirically necessary and sufficient for another is a straightforward empirical question—and in fact one which I should have thought we are already in a position to answer with a 'yes'. Surely there have as a matter of fact been cases in which a man did p in circumstances A, to bring about an end B, where his doing of p was in A both empirically necessary and sufficient for the bringing about of B. By contrast, it might be argued that the question whether there are any choices which satisfy condition (i) is not an empirical question, and that it is to metaphysics rather than to the sciences to which we must look for an answer to it. Of course we might find out, in fact already have found out, empirically that some choices do not satisfy condition (i): those in which a man chooses to do something which in his situation he is unable to do. But are there any choices which do satisfy condition (i)? Only if determinism in all of the forms I mentioned is wrong, and this is a matter for philosophy.

In any case, the views of Hume, Kant, and Peirce which Körner reminds us of, and takes to be relevant to the question he is concerned with, have no bearing on the question whether there are any choices which meet condition (iii); it is condition (i) they bear on.

I have omitted mention thus far of condition (ii), and this because (if I have understood it) it is superfluous. What it says is that a man's choice is effective only if it is *not* the case that his situation, A, empirically necessitates a situation X, which empirically necessitates a situation Y, which ... empirically necessitates the coming about of his end B, or the coming about of something incompatible with his end, thus not-B. On the assumption that the relation 'empirically necessitates' is transitive, we can abbreviate this as follows: a man's choice is effective only if it is *not* the case that A empirically necessitates B, and *not* the case that A empirically necessitates not-B. Now let us suppose that a man's choice to do p meets conditions (i) and (iii). Then, by (iii), we know that, in A, his doing p is empirically necessary and sufficient for B; hence that A can only necessitate B by necessitating p, and A can only necessitate not-B by necessitating not-p. But by (i), we know that A necessitates neither p nor not-p. Therefore A necessitates neither B nor not-B. So if a man's choice meets conditions (i) and (iii), it will also meet condition (ii).

To return, then, to condition (i). Körner's main point was that 'the assumption that there are effective choices is central to all planning'; more particularly, as I construe him, that a man who is making plans, or deliberating about what to do, assumes that his choice, whichever it will be, will be an effective choice. More particularly still, that his choice will meet condition (i). Let me pin this down as follows. Suppose it has been put to President Johnson that he should order a sea-fight to be held off the coast of China. Johnson begins to weigh reasons for and against doing this. His Secretary of State says, 'There's really no point in your doing that. For neither of the two choices you could arrive at would be an effective choice—neither would meet Professor Körner's condition (i).' Johnson replies, 'I agree that it would be pointless to deliberate about the matter if I wasn't going to be able to do what I chose; but I see no reason at all to think I won't. My mouth and lungs are in good order, and it may surely be supposed that if I choose to have a sea-fight nothing will prevent me from saying, "A sea-fight", and if I choose not to have a sea-fight nothing will prevent me from saying, "No sea-fight".' And the

S. of S. replies, 'Ah, but that takes us only half-way. For next it would have to be shown that your situation won't necessitate your saying whichever it is that you do say. That's the hard part.'

Why should anyone think that if what he does (whichever it is) will have been empirically necessitated, then it is pointless to deliberate about what to do? There are many who would agree with Körner on this. He quotes Peirce, for example, as having said that if we accept necessitarianism 'our notion that we decide what we are going to do is reduced to illusion', and if no man ever really decides what to do why bother deliberating about what to do? But it is hard to see precisely why this could be thought to be the case.

It seems to me two things at any rate are behind it. The first argument contains the very same fallacy as lies behind fatalism. The fatalist argues that if there will be a sea-fight tomorrow, then there will be one no matter what anybody does, in which case doing anything to bring it about or prevent it is pointless. On the other hand, if there will be no sea-fight tomorrow, then there will be none no matter what anybody does, in which case doing anything to bring it about or prevent it is pointless. But either there will be one or there will not be one; hence doing anything to bring about or prevent a sea-fight tomorrow is pointless. One way of describing the fallacy is this: the fact that *if* there will be a sea-fight tomorrow then there will be one no matter what anybody does today is compatible with its being the case that there will be one tomorrow if and only if somebody does something (e.g., order one laid on) today, and hence compatible with its being far from pointless to do that thing today if you want to have a sea-fight tomorrow. And similarly for the other leg of the argument. So it was a mistake to think the conclusion followed.

Consider now one way in which people have argued that we had better say that actions are not caused—in Körner's terminology 'empirically necessitated'. To begin with, the point is made that a man's thoughts, wants, choices, reasons, etc., are not the causes of any of his actions. (I shall not discuss this claim.) Then it is said: let us assume I will raise my arm. If we say that this will have a cause, we must grant that its cause will be something other than my thoughts, wants, choices, etc. So I will raise my arm whatever may be my thoughts, wants, choices, etc. So I will raise my arm whether I choose to raise it or not. But surely it is absurd to suppose that I here and now will raise my arm whether I choose to raise it or not.[1] (And have we not already ruled out that Johnson will say, 'A sea-fight' whether he chooses to have one or not? For we said that if he chooses to have none, nothing will prevent him from saying, 'No sea-fight' instead.)

Moreover, this would make deliberation pointless. For if a man supposed he will raise his arm (or keep it down) whether he chooses to or not, then why deliberate with a view to making a choice?

It *is* absurd to suppose that I here and now will raise my arm whether I choose to raise it or not. (And it may be equally absurd to suppose that Johnson will say, 'A sea-fight' whether he chooses to have one or not.) But it is not absurd—indeed, it is tautological —to suppose that *if* I will raise it I will raise it whether I choose to or not. To establish that it is not necessary to say anything whatever about causality. But that is all the argument entitles anyone to, for it began with the assumption that I will raise my arm. Moreover (cf. fatalism), 'If I will raise my arm I will raise it whether I choose to or not' is compatible with 'I will raise it if and only if I choose to'. That my raising it (if I raise it) will have been caused by something other than the choice I make does not in the slightest show that it would be false to say, 'I will raise it if and only if I choose to'. And if I know that this is true of me, and it is a weighty matter whether I raise my arm or not, it will be far from pointless for me to deliberate with a view to making a choice.

One other interesting point to notice about the argument I have been considering is that a consistent use of it would embarrass the very people who put it forward. For one could argue in the very same way as follows. 'Let us assume my arm will go up. Then it will go up whatever my thoughts, wants, choices, etc. may be. So my arm will go up whether I choose to do anything about the matter or not. And what point would there be in deliberating? So to avoid these absurdities, we had better say that bodily movements do not have causes—or at any rate those bodily movements which are "involved" in actions.' But the writers I have in mind do not really want to draw this conclusion. They wish to say that one's arm's going up, indeed, one's bodily movements generally,

[1] I believe this is behind the argument of pp. 34 and 41–42 of Charles Taylor's *The Explanation of Behavior*.

are caused. They wish to say that it is, not bodily movements, but actions which are not caused.

A second source of the view which Körner is opting for seems to me to be this. If my raising my arm had a cause, then *I* didn't do it—whatever it was, whether a psychological or physiological occurrence, that did the causing was what did the raising of the arm. *My* agency drops out; I am victim rather than agent.[2] And of course if I am not myself going to be raising my arm or keeping it down, then what point could there be in deliberating as to whether to raise it or keep it down?

A man could raise his right arm by picking it up with his left hand, or by pressing a button which closes an electrical circuit which causes his arm to go up. But in such a case his raising his arm isn't caused by his pressing the button; pressing the button is how, the means by which, he raises his arm, and not the cause of his raising it. Pressing the button can be said to be the cause of his arm's going up, but this the writers I have in mind would say is a very different matter. Nothing causes his raising of his arm.

But why? Because if a man's raising his arm has a cause, then *he* doesn't raise it. But what can this mean? It doesn't really seem to say anything more than that his raising his arm *can't* have a cause; and if so, it is not an argument, but just a re-statement of the point to be made.

It does seem reasonable to say that if a light's going on was caused by the flipping of a switch, then I didn't turn on the light unless I flipped the switch. If a gust of wind flipped the switch, then the gust of wind, not I, turned on the light; the gust of wind was agent. So perhaps one may be tempted to pass by analogy to: if my arm's going up just now was caused by a prior neural occurrence in my brain, then I didn't raise my arm unless I 'did' (performed? produced?) the prior neural occurrence in my brain. But surely I didn't 'do' the neural occurrence—to say so doesn't even make sense. And I didn't produce it either.[3] So if my arm's going up was caused by a prior neural occurrence in my brain, then I didn't raise my arm. Whatever produced that prior neural occurrence—e.g., a certain stimulus—raised my arm. *It* was the agent; not me.

[2] Cf. A. I. Melden, *Free Action*, pp. 7–9.
[3] For fear of the conclusion which is going to come, Professor Chisholm says that I do produce the occurrences in my brain. Cf. his 'Freedom and Action' in *Freedom and Determinism*, ed. Keith Lehrer.

But the writers I have in mind do not really want to draw this conclusion. For by contraposition, it yields that if I did raise my arm, my arm's going up was not caused by a prior neural occurrence in my brain. And they wish to say, as I mentioned above, that bodily movements are caused. Only actions are to have no causes. Hence they themselves cannot support their claim by appeal to this analogy, and in fact must reject it.

To say the analogy leads to an unacceptable conclusion, and hence does not go through is one thing; to explain why is another. *Why* do we say in some cases that the man did the thing, but in others that it (the wind, an electrical impulse, another person, and so on) did it? I shall not even try to answer this question. In any case, doing so could give no aid to those who say that actions have no causes—so far as I can see, it would be entirely irrelevant to that point.

One might, alternatively, try to support the claim about agency by appeal to the claim I discussed above. I.e., one might say that if my raising my arm will have a cause then *I* won't be raising it because if it has a cause then it will have a cause other than my choice, and hence will happen whether or not I choose—and how can it be an *action* of *mine* if it will come about whether or not I choose? But the trouble with the premise has already been pointed to.

In sum, it is not plain what there can be in the claim that if my raising my arm has a cause, then *I* don't raise it—more than just the insistence that my raising my arm can't have a cause. If there is nothing more in it, then Körner's view that deliberation presupposes that actions are not empirically necessitated gets no more support from this claim than it did from the claim (discussed above) that if a man's action will have a cause he will do it whether or not he chooses.

But in one way this has been very unfair. The two arguments which I have found outside Körner's paper are not given by him in his paper, and it may very well be that he could re-state them more convincingly, or that he would reject them outright and offer something else instead. So my brief critical remarks will have had some use after all if they persuade him to return to this topic again and explain in more detail why he holds this view, as well as the others in his paper which I have drawn attention to and raised questions about.

BERNARD WILLIAMS

I should like to start with one or two criticisms of more detailed points in Körner's paper. I shall then consider certain ambiguities in the formulation of determinism in the paper, with respect to the existence of choices; and here I shall go off into a brief and inconclusive excursion into the connections between determinism, choice and consciousness. I shall then advance a rather rash argument to suggest the compatibility of determinism with the existence of choices, and certainly of choices which are, in a sense relevant to planning, effective. I end by suggesting that there is something very odd about Körner's central thesis.

1. Körner says, in his terminology, that the choice of an agent in situation A to bring about B by bodily conduct p is effective if (but not only if) Ap selemp B; and Ap selemp B if the following conditions are satisfied:

(i) it is not the case that A emp p, nor that A emp p̄;
(ii) in the sequence A . . . B, B is not connected with A by one or more 'emp's;
(iii) Ap emp B.

This is an abbreviation of Körner's own statement of the conditions, in particular in leaving out the contributions to the analysis of 'Ap selemp B̄', which Körner pursues in parallel. I assume, however, that both the conjuncts of (i) are essential to the analysis of each 'selemp' proposition, both that which leads to B and that which leads to B̄. For certainly the truth of the second conjunct must be, on anyone's showing, a necessary condition of the effectiveness of a choice to bring about anything by behaviour p in situation A; and that the truth of the first conjunct is equally a necessary condition I take to be a central point of Körner's thesis.

Indeed, it might be thought that this is so much so that the first conjunct only serves to underline a point made elsewhere, and that it is entailed by conditions (ii) and (iii). Whether this is so, however, depends on two points which are not entirely clear to me: the meaning of 'connected' in condition (ii), and the relations of p to A and B in the sequence Ap B. The most natural way of taking 'connected' seems to be this: that in the sequence A . . . B, B will be connected with A by one or more 'emps' if and only if every term in the sequence A . . . B has the relation 'emp' to any term that immediately follows it. If this interpretation is correct, then the only case in which A and B are connected by one 'emp'— a possibility mentioned—will be the case in which A and B are the only terms of the sequence, which does not appear to be a case with which Körner is concerned, since it eliminates p. Leaving that, however, we may ask: is this interpretation too strong? Certainly there is an alternative weaker than this which it does not look as though Körner could have in mind, namely that B shall be said to be connected to A by one or more 'emps' if at least one 'emp' occurs somewhere in the sequence; for condition (iii) would seem itself to violate this, and the conditions would be inconsistent. Since there seems to be no suggestion of an interpretation intermediate between these two, it looks as though we should go for the strong one; and this has the (hardly calamitous) result that the first conjunct of (i) is formally redundant, at least if p is genuinely a term of the sequence A . . . B, and if 'emp' is transitive. On these assumptions, the falsity of 'A emp p' will be entailed by the satisfaction of conditions (ii) and (iii).

2. It may be, however, that what Körner is getting at by condition (ii) is rather that B should not be joined to A by 'emps' *indepedently of p*; or—another way, perhaps, of putting rather the same thing—that *Ap emp B* is to be taken as a sequence which does not have A as first term, but rather the complex item Ap. His thought then would be that it is a condition of effective choice to bring about B by behaviour p that B should not be necessitated by the situation independently of the behaviour. The motivation of this might seem to be the idea that for this choice to be effective, the behaviour p should be a necessary condition of the outcome's occurring. But if this is the intention of the condition, it seems excessively strong.

Suppose that I, being an unscrupulous politician, choose in a troubled situation to bring about the destruction of my opponent by blowing up his house; and that at the instant that I push the plunger, which is efficiently connected to sufficient explosives, the agents of another faction push their plunger, also efficiently connected to sufficient explosives (perhaps, indeed, by some operatic misapprehension, to the same explosives). I suppose that lawyers could argue whether I, or the others, either or both, had brought about this man's death or the destruction of his house.

But in the terms that are at the centre of Körner's discussion, it does not seem very realistic to insist that in such a case my choice proved *ineffective*. It would have been ineffective, surely, only if I had been prevented; and in the case described, the intervention of the others would have prevented me—as etymology suggests—only if they had got there first.

The same point would arise with even greater force if a similar interpretation were put on the requirements of the probability formulation. But I shall not pursue the probability formulation in detail: except merely to remark that in its condition (i) we do not have, as one might expect from the *emp* conditions (which are otherwise parallel), the requirement that it be false that A prob p and that A prob p̄, but rather the requirement that it be false that A prob B, and that A prob B̄. This seems to suggest strongly the 'no independent route' doctrine, and the difficulties of this in this case seem, as I first said, even more severe. It is familiar enough that a situation in which one person chooses to assassinate a political figure may well be a situation which makes it highly probable that he will be assassinated by somebody, and this fact can hardly by itself show to be ineffective the choice of that man who actually chooses to assassinate him and does so. A lot here obviously turns on the descriptions that are offered of A and B, and how specific they are.

Thus I think that there are certain difficulties both in the details of Körner's formulation, and in a view which might plausibly be taken as providing the motivation for some of that formulation. The latter difficulties can be summed up by saying: (a) it scarcely seems a sufficient condition of my choice's being ineffective in a given situation that the outcome would have resulted even if I had not acted as I in fact chose to act; (b) still less, is it a sufficient condition of my choice's being ineffective that the situation is such as to make it probable that the outcome I choose will, in any case, be the outcome.

However, it may be replied to these difficulties that they assume that the opposite of a choice's being effective in a given situation is its being ineffective in that situation; but that this is not what is intended. The opposite, rather, is the choice's *not being effective* in the situation. While it does seem a bit odd in the house explosion case, to say that my choice was ineffective, since this implies (as I suggested) that I was somehow prevented, one might say that my choice was not effective, in the sense that the behaviour I chose was not *the effective item* in bringing about the outcome. While this could be said, it does not in fact get us very far. For it seems to be true only in a rather boring sense: viz. that we cannot speak of my behaviour as *the* effective item, because there was another equally effective item. If we infer from this that my chosen behaviour was in no way effective, we are likely to get into trouble; any reason we have for saying this about my chosen behaviour in the case described, we have also for saying it in the case of the other parties' behaviour as well, and if nobody's chosen behaviour was in any way effective, it starts to look mysterious how the explosion happened at all. Surely it would be wrong to try to push the word 'effective' too hard in this case: the outcome was causally over-determined, and we understand that well enough.

3. In any case, this whole aspect of the question is perhaps of secondary importance. For no one presumably is going to deny that people's behaviour is often causally effective in bringing about certain outcomes in the world, in the sense that their behaviour is both a causally necessary condition of the outcome, and, the situation being what it is, a causally sufficient condition. Now if there are any choices at all, there are certainly choices to bring about such outcomes by means of such behaviour: (I shall not quarrel with Körner about this, perhaps not totally natural, formulation). Someone might suggest that the effectiveness of a choice consisted just in this: that the outcome I chose to bring about by certain behaviour is actually brought about by that behaviour, and not by anything else. On this suggestion, it is quite certain that if there are any choices, then there are some effective choices.

It does not seem, however, that this suggestion is acceptable to Körner, nor does it express what he means by the effectiveness of choice. For he says that it is empirically undecidable whether there are effective choices or not, and I don't *think* that he means by that that it is empirically undecidable whether there are choices or not. I am not totally clear why he says that it is empirically undecidable whether there are effective choices or not, but I take it that it is, at least primarily, because there are no conclusive falsification procedures for statements of the form 'A emp p'; similar considerations presumably apply to 'prob' formulations.

One might always find eventually that the effective behaviour just followed empirically from the situation. What is the motivation for saying that if this turned out to be so, there was no effective choice? Well, it might then seem that the choice had been by-passed and played no real role in the outcome. How?

Körner paraphrases a determinist who claims that there is no sense to the concept of effective choice, as claiming that 'chosen bodily conduct which is not empirically necessitated or empirically probabilified by its spatio-temporal antecedents is inconceivable except as a miracle'. This, then, is the determinist's objection to the possibility of the existence of effective choices. But it does not emerge very clearly from this which of two different positions this determinist is supposed to be taking. He may (a) be making the strong claim that if the spatio-temporal antecedents of bodily conduct empirically necessitate or probabilify this conduct, then such necessitation or probabilification cannot conceivably run via a choice, i.e. that the laws expressing these relations cannot themselves employ the concept of choice, or some equivalent to it, nor in any way refer to choices. Alternatively (b) he may merely be saying that even though the laws may run through choices, if they do run through choices the truth of the laws shows those choices not to be in some basic sense effective choices. On the first of these positions, if the supposed necessities actually obtained, I suppose it *might* be said that there weren't *really* any choices at all; this is a point I shall come back to.

The former of these two assumptions is not very easy to discuss; but it must be said that if the range of interpretation of probabilification is left wide, it seems on the probability interpretation at least pretty implausible. For if there were well-founded probability statements about human behaviour, there seems very little reason why they should not take the form of saying that in a certain situation it is highly probable that a given agent will choose one course of action rather than another. Nor, under this sort of interpretation, does there seem very much to commend the second position, either; for in any sense of 'effective' which is relevant, as Körner wants, to practical planning, the fact that such probability statements were true would seem to have no tendency to eliminate the effectiveness of choice. A business man who in any relevant sense works on the assumption of the existence of effective choices would be in no way put out, it seems to me, by being persuaded that it was a law of psychology that there was a very high probability that a business man in his situation with his background and personality would choose as he chooses. He may have good reason for believing this already; particularly if he has been to business school.

However, perhaps this is not the sort of probability that Körner has in mind; he may rather have in mind the sort of probability statements that occur in *physical* theory. And similarly we might, though we are not forced to, assume that any necessitation that he has in mind is necessitation in terms of a physical theory; i.e. that the determinism he is discussing is not just determinism, but some sort of physicalist determinism. Whether or not this is Körner's intention, it seems to me at least a realistic way to approach the subject on the *determinist* side, which is what I shall from now on stick to. For the belief in the possibility of a basically psychological determinism, that is to say, in the possibility of comprehensive laws predictive of human behaviour in the context of an irreducibly psychological theory, is surely a belief in magic: it is something like the belief that one could succeed in correlating the output of the organism with its input in terms of a theoretical model which perhaps had no embodiment at all, and that can scarcely be right. But that topic I shall leave.

4. However, even if we now leave probabilistic interpretations of any kind on one side; and indeed leave on one side deterministic theories whose laws run through choices so—or roughly so—specified; and we concentrate on the strongest possible case of a deterministic theory, viz. a totally physicalist deterministic theory: we are still left with the problem of where it leaves whatever it is we normally call choice. I suggested earlier that if the strong physicalist determinism came to light, someone might say that there weren't *really* any choices at all. Now I admit that it isn't totally clear what the force or content of this suggestion would be; and this is in some part for the well-known reason that we are not in a position in the philosophy of mind to be at all clear what the relations could be between such a physicalist account and our common psychological vocabulary. But I suppose that part of its force could be caught in this way: that we speak of computors and similar machines making choices, and selecting, deciding, etc., but have a strong desire to put quotes round these expressions, as only analogously or half-heartedly applying to

what goes on in these machines. However, it may be objected that this consideration could not conceivably move us, whatever laws were discovered, to say that human beings did not really make choices; for—it will be said—the basic reason that we hesitate in the application of these expressions to these machines is that the machines are not conscious, while we are. But the uncovering of physical determinism as applying to human beings could not *abolish* the fact that we are conscious; hence it could not conceivably provide the reason in the case of human beings which is the reason in the case of the machines for hesitating to say that they make choices.

However, this rather blank consideration does not really shed much light on the situation. For now it can be said, either the fact that we are conscious—whatever fact that may be—makes a difference in the way *we* work from the ways in which our present machines work—that is to say, indisputably machine-like machines —or it does not make any difference. Suppose it does not. Then we can say, if we like, that it remains true that we make choices, even under physical determinism, and the simple machines don't, just because we are conscious—even under physical determinism —while they are not. But there wouldn't be much point in insisting on it. For what we are insisting on, as things are, in making this distinction might well be thought, if it has anything to do with consciousness, to have something to do with the idea that being conscious makes a difference, and, on the present supposition, it is supposed not to make any difference. So in this case we could say, with point, that we had discovered that there were not any choices; we should be registering by that the very surprising fact that consciousness did not make any difference. This would be so surprising that we should perhaps try the other supposition, surely the correct one, that it does make a difference; i.e. that there is an important difference in the performances, internal states, input-processing, etc. of things that are conscious compared with those of things that are not. If this is so, the difference must itself show up in the physical determinist theory; for such a theory, being ex hypothesi comprehensive, must account for everything that actually makes a difference. In this case, we might hold on, with some point, to saying that physical determinism *had not* shown that we do not make choices, in so far as that question turns on the issue of our being conscious, which is the present focus of the discussion. For the two necessary conditions of the application of the concept of choice which are at issue are (1) that it goes with consciousness and (2) that consciousness makes a difference; and both of these conditions could be satisfied under physical determinism, if physical determinism is possible at all. But of course we must now notice that in agreeing to this, we have weakened the position with which we started in introducing physical determinism: viz. that the laws of such determinism would not run through choices. For it now looks as though they could run through something very like choices, while still being laws of physical determinism.

All this last bit arose out of an attempt to connect choice specifically with consciousness. Now of course it is always possible for someone to leave the appeal to consciousness altogether and just claim: if physical determinism, no choices, i.e., if behaviour is chosen, then it is not physically caused.

But just as a blank claim, this does not really look very appetising. It needs argument; and that argument presumably must not rest specifically on connecting choice with consciousness, if the previous very sketchy considerations were in the right direction; for they suggested that on the more plausible alternative, there could well be a point in saying that the existence of choices was compatible with physical determinism, if physical determinism is possible at all.

5. After these rather inconclusive considerations I should now like to advance a stronger line here, which will at least provide a challenge to anyone defending what I called the blank claim; and also lead back to one of Körner's central ideas. The stronger line consists in directly claiming that the existence of choices, in any sense in which people wish to defend this, must be compatible with physical (and *a fortiori* any other form of determinism), if the truth of determinism can be regarded as at all an open question. For, in any sense in which people wish to defend the idea that we make choices, it must be certain that we make choices now; for what they are doing is *defending*—they do not want any *more* than we have got. But if determinism is true, it is true *now*; and if it is true now, it must be compatible with anything that is true now. And one thing that is certainly true now is that we make choices in the sense in which people want to defend this. So if determinism were incompatible with the making of choices in this sense, we

could know that determinism was false, and the truth of determinism would not be an open question. So it it is at all an open question, its truth must be compatible with the making of choices.[1]

To this it may be said that it is not certain that in the required sense we make choices; perhaps we do not (i.e. if determinism is true). But it really is not in the least clear why we should want *more*; in any case it can certainly be said that if we *don't* in fact make choices as things are, the non-choices that do go on seem enough to satisfy practically anyone's appetite for choice. So perhaps the objection is rather that if we *knew* that determinism was true, we should stop making choices in the sense that we do now make them. But why? would this be a merely causal result of the knowledge of determinism? This seems unlikely; and even if it were true, it seems at least equally likely that we should get over it, e.g. by our desire for choice causing us to forget the truth of determinism. Perhaps, then, the knowledge of determinism will give us *reasons* for abandoning choice: (not taking a 'reason' necessarily to be other than a special sort of cause). This is even more absurd; for, first, the reason would presumably be a reason for *choosing* to abandon choice, and a little reflection on that should establish that the reason can scarcely be a very good reason for so doing; and second, the reason could really only consist in some conviction that choice is incompatible with determinism, and anyone among those future persons who has heard of or thought of my argument will be able to see that that conviction is misguided, i.e. that he has not got a good reason.

This may be thought rather a drastic line. But whatever is thought of it, at least the following seems plausible; the existence of choices in a sense relevant to *planning* is compatible with determinism, if the truth of determinism is at all an open question. For certainly we plan; so if any choices are relevant to planning, they are, on occasion, available to us. So, by a more restricted version of my previous argument, if determinism is at all an open question, it is compatible with this state of affairs. If so, there must surely be something very odd about Körner's position.

---

[1] It is not a consequence of this that determinism, if an open question at all, is compatible with free will. It might well be the case that under determinism there were choices, but no *free* choices, where 'free choice' is a notion particularly associated with ideas we now have about responsibility, blame, efforts of will, etc. The claim that these ideas could remain largely undisturbed by one's coming to know that determinism was true seems to me wildly implausible.

What I have been discussing in terms of the existence of choices, is surely in some part what he discusses in terms of whether there are effective choices. If, as he claims, and as is central to his argument, the policies of a person who accepts that there are effective choices differ from the policy of one who does not, this surely can be rationally so only because that person believes the following: that what happens if there are effective choices differs from what happens if there are not. But surely in any sense in which that is true, what happens now is what happens when there are effective choices. If so, then if determinism is an open question, it is compatible with those happenings. But Körner clearly believes that determinism is an open question; for when he says that it is empirically undecidable he obviously does not mean that it is decidable, only not empirically so. So I think he should accept that it is compatible with what actually goes on, and hence that the policy decision does not get off the ground.

Apart from this, there are two odd features of the policy decision itself, which partly parallel, perhaps, oddnesses I suggested earlier in the supposed consequences of our discovering determinism to be true. First, what is the content of the pessimistic policy based on the assumption that there are no effective choices? Not making any choices? If so, this man will at the very least get less than he gets now. So he will be getting less than he does get now in a situation which is ex hypothesi compatible with determinism. And this does not show, as Körner argues, that it would be a silly policy; it shows that the idea that what we are confronted with here is a choice of policies is based on a confusion.

Second, how can this person suppose that he can *choose* the pessimistic policy? For once more, it must occur to him that either he can choose a policy and make a difference, or he cannot. If he can, then not only all support for the pessimistic policy disappears, but so also does all support for the idea that what he is confronted with, in face of the possibility of determinism, is Körner's choice of policies; for if he can choose effectively enough to choose this deeply drastic policy, then he can choose effectively enough: whatever is the case with determinism. If on the other hand, he can't choose a policy, he can't choose between the policies. So either way he must surely realise that he is not confronted with Körner's choice of policies.

Reply

S. KÖRNER

In this Reply I shall try to answer the main questions and objections of my critics by sketching in somewhat different words, and without technicalities, the main aim and structure of my argument.

1. The dominant philosophical accounts of situations in which a person seems to be faced with the possibility of realizing by suitably chosen bodily conduct one of at least two options, each of which is realizable in the course of nature are (i) the 'grand-illusion-theory': at most one of the options is realizable in nature; (ii) the 'double-world-theory': although at most one option is realizable in nature, more than one option is *somehow* realizable outside it; (iii) the 'double-language-theory': there is no inconsistency between asserting the realizability of at most one option in a 'physical' and of more than one option in a 'mental' language. Of these accounts the first has been worked out in the British empiricist tradition, the second in the philosophies of Plato and Kant, the third to some extent by some recent philosophers, e.g. H. Feigl. My aim is to take some steps towards working out a fourth thought-possibility, according to which we, occasionally, realize by suitably chosen bodily behaviour one of at least two equally realizable options.

2. Let us call any spatio-temporally delimited, changeable or changing, situation or state of affairs a 'situation'. A situation may include another situation, e.g. chosen bodily conduct. I shall say of a situation which is (causally or with a definite probability) determined by a preceding situation or set of situations that it is 'predetermined' by it. A situation which a person has chosen to bring about by his chosen bodily conduct will be called an 'option'. A person's chosen bodily conduct is 'effectively chosen', and his option an 'effective option', if, and only if, (a) his chosen bodily conduct (and, therefore, any situation including it) is not predetermined by the situations preceding it; (b) the situations preceding his chosen bodily conduct do not predetermine his option, which is a situation succeeding his chosen bodily conduct; (c) in conjunction with one or more situations preceding it, his chosen bodily conduct predetermines his option.[1] Since the concepts of

[1] The present statement of (b) differs slightly from that given in the paper: (a) and (b) are now clearly independent.

effectively chosen bodily conduct and of effective option have been defined in terms of 'predetermination' and 'non-predetermination' (and thus of 'open futures') the question of their emptiness or otherwise is not empirically decidable. It should be equally obvious that the question whether or not a sequence of situations 'goes through' (a situation including) chosen bodily conduct has nothing to do with the question whether or not the chosen bodily conduct is effectively chosen.

3. It is frequently asserted, especially by proponents of the grand-illusion-theory, that my chosen bodily conduct is either predetermined by situations preceding it or else occurs by pure chance. If this dichotomy were complete, then my definition of 'effectively chosen bodily conduct' and 'effective option' would, at best, be pointless. But there is a third logical possibility. Apart from the possibility that my chosen bodily conduct is predetermined (i.e. apart from the possibility that the total situation which includes my chosen bodily conduct is predetermined in all its aspects) by preceding situations, and apart from the possibility that it is happening by pure chance it might be *determined by non-situations*, e.g. Fregean thoughts, Platonic forms, the categorical imperative, etc. That the apprehension of such non-situations is itself a situation, does not exclude the possibility that a non-situation should determine (though, of course, not predetermine) the chosen bodily conduct. Suggestions about the nature of such a determination are found, e.g., in Kant's analysis of respect for the moral law and in Frege's article, quoted above. The general definition of effectively chosen bodily conduct makes room for more specific accounts of it as determined by non-situations. Chosen bodily conduct and, much more so, effectively chosen bodily conduct as determined by non-situations, such as Fregean thoughts, are reasonably ascribed to human beings and not, e.g., to maranta plants.

4. If we assume that the concept of effectively chosen bodily conduct is not empty, then we *eo ipso* restrict any principle to the effect that all situations (or, as we might also say, all total situations in all their aspects) are predetermined by situations preceding them. Such a restriction is compatible with science, as we know it, though not with scientism and some other metaphysical doctrines.

5. Some people, including myself, have the empirically undecidable belief that at some times of their life they have the

opportunity of effectively choosing between at least two different futures which are equally realizable in nature by suitably chosen bodily conduct. *If* at every time of my life my future is in all its aspects determined by my past, then at most one of my (incompatible) options is realizable—whether or not I prefer it to the others. No choice of policy and none of my beliefs could make any difference to the course of nature and my life in it. The 'pessimistic' assumption that I have at any time only one realizable future and the 'optimistic' assumption that I have at some times more than one realizable future, would be equally irrelevant to the course of my life. *If*, on the other hand, I have at some times of my life the opportunity of effectively choosing between at least two realizable futures, then the pessimistic and the optimistic assumptions could be relevant to the course of my life. Making the pessimistic assumption might, for example, serve me as an excuse to spare myself a successful effort towards realizing a preferred option which I would not spare myself, if I made the optimistic assumption.

To show that making the empirically undecidable, optimistic assumption might make a favourable difference to the achievement of preferred options, is to justify it pragmatically. If the pragmatic justification of the optimistic assumption seems "odd", the reason may well lie in a fallacious inference from the statement that I have at every time of my life only one (realized) past to the statement that I have at every time of my life only one realizable future.

www.ingramcontent.com/pod-product-compliance
Lightning Source LLC
Chambersburg PA
CBHW020418080526
44584CB00014B/1395